China's Daughters
Women Who Shaped Chinese History

Suzanne Williams
Illustrations by Amber MacLean

Pacific View Press
Berkeley, California

To all of our daughters — Ana, Lucia, Mara, and Michelle. They will write the future.

Acknowledgements

Page 26: Princess Wencheng Poem, *100 Celebrated Chinese Women,* by Cai Zhuozhi, translated by Kate Foster, Asiapac Books Pte, Ltd., Singapore, 1995 p. 79

Page 41: Li Qingzhao Poem, *http://www.chinapage.org/poet-e/liqing-e.html,* translation by Lucy Chao Ho, Seton Hall University: Internet 8/27/2010

Text and illustrations copyright © 2011
Cover design: Jos Sances, Interior design: Nancy Ippolito
All rights reserved. No part of this book may be used or reproduced, stored in a retrieval system, or transmitted, in any form or by any means, electronic, mechanical, photocopying, recording, or otherwise without prior permission in writing from the publisher. Address inquiries to Pacific View Press, P.O. Box 2897, Berkeley, CA 94702, or e-mail: *Nancy @pacificviewpress.com.* Website: *www.pacificviewpress.com*

Printed in the United States
Library of Congress Cataloging-in-Publication Data
Williams, Suzanne, 1949-
   China's daughters / Suzanne Morgan Williams; illustrations, Amber MacLean.
   p. cm.
   Includes index.
   ISBN 978-1-881896-34-0
   1. Women--China--History--Juvenile literature. 2. Women--China--Biography--Juvenile literature. 3. China--History--Juvenile literature. 4. China--Social conditions--Juvenile literature. 5. China--Biography--Juvenile literature. I. MacLean, Amber, ill. II. Title.

HQ1767.W55 2011
920.720951--dc22

2010054589

Contents

Nu Wa Makes the People 5
Fu Hao 7
    Zheng Zhenxiang, Archaeologist 8
    A Military Leader 9
    Oracle Bones 10
    The Zhou Dynasty and Patriarchy 11
    Confucius 11
Mengmu 13
Ban Zhao 17
    Three Obediences 18
    Madam Wei Shuo 19
    Learning from Books 19
Baogu 21
    Laozi 22
    Daoist Heroine 23
    Three Traditions 23
Princess Wencheng 25
    Controlling an Empire 26
    Buddhism Began in India 27
    Guanyin 29
Wu Zetian 31
    Concubines 32
    Courtesans 33
    Scholars and the Mandate of Heaven 34
    The Story of Luofu 35
Li Qingzhao 37
    Silk Weaving 39
    Marriage 40
Huang Daopo 43
    The Silk Trade 44
    Holeus 45
    Zhinu & Niulang, The Cowherd & the Weaver 47

Woman Liu, Lady Guan, and Empress Ma 49
    Footbinding 50
    Widows 51
    Temples to Empress Ma 52
    Nushu Women's Writing 53
Zhen Yuanyuan 55
    The Imperial Palace and Imperial City 56
    The Manchu 57
Hong Xuanjiao 59
    Hua Mulan 60
Cixi, the Empress Dowager 63
    Older Women 64
    Dragon and Phoenix 65
Qiu Jin 69
    Students and Revolution 70
    Sun Yatsen 71
Xiang Jingyu 73
    The Republic of China/New Culture Movement 74
    People's Nationalist Party 75
    Communist Party of China 76
    Woman Students and Revolution 77
    Women in the 1911 Revolution 77
Soong Qingling 79
    Who Supported What? 82
    World War II 84
Kang Keqing 87
    Women in the Revolution 88
    A People's Army 89
    Cultural Revolution 91
    Marriage Law 92
    Leaders 93
Moving On 94
A Folk Legend: Li Chi and the Monster 96
    The Chinese Language and Pronunciation 97
    Bibliography 98
    Index 100

Nu Wa Makes the People

According to Chinese legend the god Pan Gu created the earth. But it was the second god, Nu Wa, who created the Chinese people. Nu Wa was a woman with a snake's body. She was curious and loved everything about the earth. But she was lonely.

One day, she began to play with the yellow mud along the edge of a river. Gently, she formed little figures from the mud. She made each one different—one tall, one short, one thin, one fat. As she set them on the river bank, they came to life. Each person woke, stretched, and began to move. Nu Wa hurried to make another and another. It was such fun! She couldn't make people fast enough.

Finally, she took a branch, dipped it in the mud, and began to fling drops of mud along the river bank. Each drop turned into a man or a woman. Nu Wa threw the mud faster and faster, creating more and more people. The legend says these drops of mud became ordinary men and women, while those Nu Wa shaped with her hands received special gifts and talents.

In this way, Nu Wa, from the beginning, made men and women, common people, and a ruling class. Each had a place in China.

Fu Hao

Powerful Ancestor
Around 1200 BCE
Shang Dynasty About 1600–1046 BCE

Zheng Zhenxiang wanted to dig deeper. She was sure there was a tomb beneath the small palace. It was 1976, and the archaeologist was working at Anyang, Henan Province. She was excavating in the Yin Ruins, where eight generations of Shang dynasty kings had lived. Her team had already dug five meters (sixteen feet) down. Other archaeologists didn't believe a tomb would be found so near a palace.

Zheng disagreed. Her team kept working. They reached seven and one-half meters (twenty-four feet). Then, Zheng Zhenxiang found her prize. Her team uncovered a small tomb built to face north-south. The tomb held forty thousand objects—huge bronze vessels, seven hundred pieces of ancient jade, hairpins, mirrors, weapons, oracle bones, and shells used for money. There were the remains of a lacquered coffin. Sixteen human skeletons and the skeletons of six dogs had been placed in niches on the sides of the tomb. This was the tomb of an important person.

It was a treasure not just of things, but of information. The tomb had been sealed since the person was buried more than three thousand years before. This was the first time archaeologists had found a Shang tomb that hadn't been raided by grave robbers. Using the clues from the objects found in the tomb, they would learn more about the times of the Shang dynasty. The team carefully marked and removed the pieces for study. As they read the inscriptions on the bronzes and oracle bones, they began to realize what an important discovery this was.

Zheng Zhenxiang had found the tomb of the Shang queen, Fu Hao. Historians and archaeologists knew of Fu Hao from other oracle inscriptions and the writings of ancient historians. Now, here were her remains. And here, in her tomb, was a collection of things she would need in her next life.

Three thousand years ago today's China didn't exist. Even the land was different. Forests and swamps covered places that today have farms or deserts. But the ancestors of today's Chinese people had already been building a civilization for centuries. By Fu Hao's time, the people of central China were skillful farmers who could grow enough food to support artists, craftsmen, and their ruling class. They grew grain, irrigated their fields and worked them with metal-tipped tools. Sometimes they hunted to provide more meat for their families. They made ceramics and used horses to pull wheeled carts and chariots. Shang people raised silkworms and wove cloth from silk and hemp. They could carve graceful figures from jade. They had invented writing. And they had mastered the art of smelting bronze. Miners dug copper and tin ore. Dozens or perhaps hundreds of artisans worked together to smelt and mix the ores. They cast beautiful jewelry, weapons for Shang soldiers, and splendidly decorated large bronze vessels for royal ceremonies,

Shang people lived with groups of their male relatives. Grandfathers, fathers, and sons and their families lived and worked together. They farmed the lands of their royalty and their own small plots. Ordinary families lived in small pit houses dug into the ground. The roofs were made of straw or leaves. People slept on benches carved into the walls of the pit. They could cook over a fire in the middle. The villages bustled with children splashing as mothers bathed them, girls carrying water to start the morning meal, and little boys pinching their noses shut as they passed the smelly animal skins hanging and ready to be tanned.

Zheng Zhenxiang, Archaeologist

Fu Hao's tomb is considered one of China's most important archaeological treasures. It would probably have remained undiscovered if Zheng Zhenxiang hadn't challenged traditional scientific thinking about Shang burial customs. Zheng, the first woman archaeologist trained in New China, entered Beijing University in 1950, just one year after the founding of the People's Republic of China. In 1962, she joined the research project at the Yin Ruins (Yinxu). Here, archaeologists from the Chinese Academy of Science worked to learn more about the little-understood Shang dynasty. Zheng, who spent more than forty years in research at the Yin Ruins, said the most impressive experience of her life had been the discovery of Fu Hao's tomb.

These ordinary Shang people and Fu Hao lived very differently. Fu Hao was a queen. She was one of three wives of the king, Wu Ding, but she was the most important. Ancient Chinese royalty lived in cities, surrounded by walls made from rammed earth. Their palaces were built of wood and tile. Their storehouses were full of grain. Traders brought them spices, jewels, and gifts from their journeys. Bronze workers in the royal workshops cast ornaments for their use. Royal families relaxed in their gardens. They laughed at entertainers and marveled at dancers.

Shang royalty had special responsibilities. They made decisions about planting and storing crops. They decided when to fight neighboring tribes, and how the battles would be fought. And they made offerings to the ancestors.

Shang people believed that their own lives were affected by the ancestors of their royalty. The ancestors lived in a world much like ours. They could watch this world and had opinions about it. The Shang believed the ancestors could create floods, earthquakes, and famines. The also believed the ancestors could help the people win battles, or grow good crops. Shang people believed only their royalty could communicate with these ancestors.

One of Fu Hao's most important duties was to make ceremonial offerings to the ancestors. The offerings of kings and queens would have been serious and impressive events. Special bronze vessels, decorated with powerful animal and spirit symbols were used during these rituals. Some were for wine, and others for meat. Each word or movement of the ceremony probably had special meaning. It may have taken days or weeks to get ready. Fu Hao must have felt excited, or possibly tense, as she prepared. Did she wear her

A Military Leader
The Shang won land, resources, and slaves through war. Organizing battles was an important responsibility of Shang rulers. Fu Hao was in charge of providing soldiers from her estate. She also personally raised troops for large battles. Fu Hao may not have gone into battle herself, but she was considered a soldier and a general. Records say her troops defeated the neighboring Tu tribe. No Shang leader had been able to do this before. Like other Shang nobles, Fu Hao had slaves. They were captured from other tribes during wars. The slaves worked in her fields and household. They often didn't speak the same language. They probably didn't take part in Shang rituals or celebrations. They knew they could be traded, given away, or killed. They were expected to serve their masters in the next world, too.

finest silk robes? Did she decorate her hair with jade ornaments? Did she fast or cleanse her body before the ceremony? We don't know. But we do know that Fu Hao was a shaman as well as a queen. Many of the oracle bones found in her tomb were inscribed with the words, "Prepared by Fu Hao." In their ceremonies, shamans used oracle bones to try to learn what the ancestors were thinking. It must have been an exciting moment when the people gathered to hear the predictions. Predictions of a good crop or a season without floods could set off a celebration. Royalty gained power and authority from correctly interpreting the markings on the oracle bones.

Oracle Bones

In many traditional societies, shamans are people who are believed to be able to communicate directly with animal spirits and ancestors. During the Shang dynasty, shamans predicted the future for rulers. They heated turtle shells or shoulder blades of large animals until they cracked. Then the shamans decided what the cracks meant. Often, they engraved their predictions on the bones. In later centuries when these bones were found, they were often sold as antiques or ground into powder for medicine. In the early 1900s, archaeologists figured out what they were and learned to read the inscriptions. The oracle bones preserve China's first writing, and are important pieces in the puzzle of Shang history.

Fu Hao was a wealthy woman with her own estate. Like other Shang lords, she controlled certain lands and the people who lived there. The families on Fu Hao's estate planted her fields and harvested her crops. The men who lived there would have formed a battle unit.

When Fu Hao died, she joined other royal ancestors in the next world. She had been important and powerful during her lifetime and she would continue to shape the lives of Shang people as an ancestor. She would need servants, weapons, and symbols of power. The Shang buried her with slaves and dogs. Workers added combs and jade ornaments that a woman would need. They laid ninety battle axes and dozens of arrowheads near her because she was a warrior. Bronze vessels were made to honor her. Shamans offered predictions written on oracle bones. These were buried with her, too. It is said that after Fu Hao died, King Wu Ding prayed to her spirit before each new battle. Fu Hao had been a powerful queen. Now she was a powerful ancestor of the Shang people.

The Zhou Dynasty and Patriarchy

Around 1046 BCE, the Shang were conquered by the more powerful Zhou. Zhou kings continued the ancestor worship of the Shang, and expanded Shang social organization. Powerful nobles ruled large estates and competed for power with their large armies of peasant soldiers. Eventually, by about 481 BCE, the Zhou kingdom had split into seven warring groups, which would battle each other (the Warring States Period) until 221 BCE, when one group, the Qin, conquered the others, united the kingdom, and established the Qin dynasty. During the Zhou era, rules and customs were developing that would control both Chinese society and women's lives for centuries. This system of rules formed a patriarchy. In a patriarchy, wealth, land, and power are passed down from fathers to sons. Zhou women did not own land. When they married they went to live with their husbands' families. Husbands could divorce wives, but women could not divorce husbands. The children belonged to the husband's family. Women weren't usually educated. A woman's job was to serve her family.

Confucius (551–479 BCE)

Confucius was a court official and philosopher during the Spring and Autumn Period (780–481 BCE). Like the later Warring States Period, it was a dangerous, war-torn time. Many scholars and philosophers debated ways to improve society. Confucius longed for what he believed was the orderliness of early Zhou society. Chinese royalty had been turning to ancestors for help since Shang times. Royalty was responsible for performing special ceremonies and rites that honored their ancestors. Both royalty and the common people believed that if the royal ancestors were honored properly they could help in practical ways. The ancestors could provide good harvests and prevent rivers from flooding. They could change the weather or help with a battle. Honoring ancestors was important. It gave royalty power. The ideas of Confucius gave order to these traditions. Confucius said life was a series of relationships. Sons should obey fathers, and fathers should honor their dead ancestors. Subjects should obey rulers and servants obey masters. Women should obey men. Good people made good homes and good rulers made good government. The ideas of Confucius and his followers would guide Chinese society for more than two thousand years.

Mengmu

Ideal Mother
About 380 BCE
Warring States Period 475–221 BCE

Mengmu's husband had just died. Her young son played in the courtyard of her in-laws' home. This had been Mengmu's home too, but that was about to change. She knew she had lost more than her husband. When he died, she lost her home and security as well. China, after the Zhou dynasty, was a difficult place for anyone to live. It must have been terrifying for a poor widow facing life on her own.

The Zhou kingdom, which followed the Shang, had collapsed. No single person or family ruled the Chinese people. Noblemen and generals fought fierce battles to gain control of more land and people. Villagers could be caught in the conflict. Their homes might be burned, or their livestock killed. A strong family could provide protection in wartime. Married Chinese women lived with their husband's families. The household might include grandparents and two or three adult brothers along with their wives and children. But now Mengmu was a widow.

We don't know why, but Mengmu and her son moved away from her husband's family. Perhaps the family couldn't afford to support her after her husband died. Maybe she had never gotten along with her mother-in-law. Or, possibly, she ran away because the family arranged a second marriage for her that she refused to accept. We know only that Mengmu was alone in dangerous times with a young son to care for.

How could Mengmu feed herself and her son? Since Zhou times, women couldn't own land. Mengmu had no land to farm. She could become a servant, but that life was hard. She might not be able to keep her son with her. The family she worked for could make her do whatever it pleased. Almost anything would be better than becoming a servant.

A widow like Mengmu couldn't just go find a job. China had grown larger and life was more complex than in Shang times. But most people were still farmers. Women did the same types of work they had always done. Farm women tended pigs and chickens. They carried water and wood. They wove cloth from hemp or silk and made the family's clothes and shoes. They helped with planting and harvesting. In towns, some families might have had a small shop, or specialized in making pottery, bronze, or lacquerware. A few women probably helped with those tasks. Women, on farms and in towns, took care of babies, children, and old people. As girls, they worked for their parents. Then they married and served their husband, his parents, and his children.

What Mengmu knew how to do was weave. She took her young son, Mencius, to a town. Towns had walls, and possibly a nobleman's troops, for protection. She must have found a place for them to stay. Perhaps she traded weaving for a room in a family's house, or rented a room next to a small shop. Then she began to weave. She wove hemp and silk and sold it so they could eat. Weaving took hours. It took patience. But it was a respectable job for a woman.

Mengmu had another worry. What would happen to her son? Chinese families passed on their land to their sons. There would be no farm for her son to inherit. It was unlikely he could become an artisan. Those skills were passed down through families, too. Somehow, Mengmu had to prepare him for the future. She had a vision. He would be a scholar!

The best way for a Chinese man to help his family was to get an education. Educated men advised the noble families. They kept records. They collected taxes and administered laws. An educated man could earn a good living. His family could get ahead.

It cost money to send a boy to school, but Mengmu was determined. She wouldn't just survive. She would give her son the future she wanted him to have. She wove late into the night, to earn enough money so Mencius could go to school. When she couldn't weave enough, she borrowed money to buy a better, faster, loom. She imagined Mencius as a scholar. But he was a child, and he acted like a child.

Mencius would rather play than study. Mengmu often found him in a graveyard with his friends. One day she saw the children playing "mourner." They wailed and tore at their clothes. This was no way for him to act. Mengmu decided to move. She found a place near a market. The market place, with its piles of vegetables, cages of squawking chickens, and people yelling and bargaining, was an exciting playground. Now, Mengmu worried about what her son would learn from people like chicken farmers, jugglers, tea vendors, and scrap dealers. They were common people. She wanted her son to make something more of himself. Mengmu must have been angry. Was she weaving until her back ached so he could learn bad language from butchers and thieves? She told him he must study hard and stay away from the market. But he refused to listen.

Mengmu had to do something. She decided to move again, to a quieter neighborhood. It probably wasn't easy for a poor widow to find a better place to live. But she managed to find a room near a school. Still, Mencius didn't study hard.

One legend says that Mengmu took her scissors and cut the beautiful piece of silk she was weaving in half. Horrified, Mencius asked, "Why did you ruin the cloth?"

Mengmu replied, "Your studies are like the cloth. One thread holds the next. If you break the threads, the cloth is ruined. If you don't go to school and study every day, your education will be ruined." After that, Mencius studied harder.

Mencius did become a good student. In time, he studied the ideas of Confucius and wrote his own commentaries. He became a famous scholar and philosopher. When Chinese people remember Mencius, they remember his great ideas, but they also remember his mother. For many centuries, Mengmu has been admired as the ideal Chinese woman, a mother who struggled and sacrificed for her son.

Ban Zhao

Confucian Scholar
48–117 CE
Han Dynasty 206 BCE*–220* CE

From the beginning, Ban Zhao's life was special. She was born into a scholar's family and raised in a comfortable, cultured home. Ban Zhao didn't have to work in the fields or worry about where her food would come from. She led a privileged life. In some ways, her childhood would have been like most girls' lives during the Han dynasty. She learned to sew and weave, to cook and care for children. But Ban Zhao's family also taught her to read and write. Ban Zhao's father was a famous historian. He had at least one son to carry on his life's work, but he also educated his daughter.

In Han times, and for centuries afterwards, most Chinese families worked hard to educate boys. Only scholars were likely to educate their daughters, too. But a girl's education was different from her brother's. Boys went to school with other boys. Girls were tutored at home. Boys were educated to run the empire. Girls learned to be wives of cultured men. Girls were taught some reading and writing, and to recite poetry, sing, and play musical instruments.

Ban Zhao may not have liked the hours of practice it took to learn her characters any more than her brothers did. She may have tired of memorizing and studying history and classic texts written by philosophers like Confucius and Mencius. But Ban Zhao had opportunities few Chinese women could imagine. Most girls didn't study these texts.

Why did Ban Zhao's father decide she should study like her brothers? Perhaps she was exceptionally intelligent. Maybe he wanted to pass on the family tradition to all of his children. There is no way to know. But he probably didn't do it to challenge the Han government's Confucian ideas about women.

Ban Zhao's father and brothers were exactly the kind of men who could get ahead during Han times. They were part of an elite, educated class who served the empire by thinking, reading, and writing. Educated men kept records and represented the government in the countryside. Some were advisors to the court. They would not question the ideas that allowed men to advance through their abilities and usefulness to the court. So, Ban Zhao was raised believing Confucian ideas, including the ones that said women should serve men.

Ban Zhao's father was writing the *Book of Han (Hanshu)*, which is still today considered a major work of Chinese history. It describes the first three hundred years of the Han dynasty. After his death, Ban Zhao's brother continued their father's work. When her brother died, it was Ban Zhao who finished collecting information and writing the book. Besides completing the *Book of Han*, she wrote or coauthored many other books. She is best known for *Lessons for Women (Nujie)*. It reflected her Confucian background, calling for women to be educated so they could live and serve as good Confucian wives. It says:

Three Obediences
During Han times many Confucian ideas became law. Confucius said women should learn "three obediences." They should obey their fathers in childhood, their husbands in marriage, and their sons when widowed. A woman couldn't own land, or question her husband, father, or son. A husband could beat his wife without punishment, but a wife could be punished for arguing too much with her husband. In Han China, women were supposed to obey decisions made by the men in their lives. Ban Zhao lived under these laws.

"Women should be humble and industrious. Men and women should marry. Men study because their position is to be masters. Women should be taught to read and write too, so they can carry out their position to serve.

"Wives must not scold and nag. Husbands must not beat their wives. A woman should be careful and modest, choose her words carefully, and keep herself clean. She should work at sewing, weaving, preparing wine and food, and serving guests.

"Although a man can remarry, a devoted wife does not. She should obey her parents-in-law, whether she agrees with them or not, and try to get along with other family members. This honors her husband."

Ban Zhao was such a respected historian that she was often summoned to the emperor's court to lecture to other, male, scholars. When Ban Zhao's husband died, the emperor called on her to move to the imperial court to teach the empress and other court women. Ban Zhao found herself in the center of court life. Her ideas were accepted in the highest circles. *Lessons for Women* became regular reading for girls educated by their families. Ban Zhao's ideas influenced the education of Chinese women until modern times.

Madam Wei Shuo (272–349 CE)

In Chinese culture, calligraphy, creating beautiful characters with a brush and ink, is an art. The form and feeling of characters adds to their meaning. It takes years of study to become a great calligrapher. Madam Wei's grandfather and uncle were both calligraphers. When she was a girl, she wanted to study calligraphy too, but that wasn't what girls did. Young Madam Wei was determined. She watched her relatives work and she practiced in her room. One day, her uncle found some of her writing. He decided she was talented and should be allowed to learn. In time, her family arranged for a well-known calligrapher to tutor her. Madam Wei created her own special style and teaching methods. Even today, students of calligraphy follow her system, practicing seven basic brush strokes and learning big characters before small ones. She is still honored as the teacher of Wang Xizhi, the finest calligrapher of his day.

Learning from Books

In China, writing with characters began during Shang times. By the Han dynasty, books existed, written on bamboo strips or silk. The early Chinese recorded history, scientific, and astronomical observations. They also wrote poetry and songs. Scholars, nobles, and emperors built libraries and collected texts. Many of these old books no longer exist. We know about them because scholars from the Han and later dynasties referred to or quoted from them.

Baogu

Daoist Doctor
304–64
Jin Dynasty 265–420

Baogu grew up in mountainous Guangdong Province. Her father, Bao Qian, was a Jin dynasty official. He was also a Daoist and an expert doctor. He probably learned about medicine from his own father. Bao Qian taught his daughter, Baogu, medicine. While other girls were weaving or threshing grain, Baogu took long walks in the forest with her father. She learned the names and the uses of plants and herbs. She learned how to mix teas to treat a cough or an upset stomach. Baogu may have learned some things from books, but most of her knowledge came from helping her father. She would have memorized formulas for medicines. She learned to crush herbs between her fingers and sniff them to see if they were still fresh. She practiced examining a patient's tongue, reading it for signs of illness while her father watched. She asked him questions about the pulses she felt along a person's wrist.

In Baogu's time, most people learned what they needed to know this way. They watched, practiced, and memorized. Baogu would have also learned stories of gods, monsters, kingdoms, and heroes by listening to older people. When her village prepared for the New Year's celebration, she would have memorized the recipes for sweet cakes, and the way to hang lanterns. In the spring, she probably helped older relatives clean her family's graves, learning the prayers to say and practicing how to make offerings to ancestors.

As Baogu practiced healing, she may have thought more about the bones she was learning to set than about the tradition she carried on. But when she learned medicine from her father, she became part of an ancient Daoist tradition. Daoism grew out of the religion of the Shang and Zhou kingdoms. It honors many spirits, gods, and village deities, and incorporates folk knowledge and belief. Some Daoists became experts at practical things such as medicine, martial arts, or predicting the future.

The medical knowledge Baogu's father shared with her had been collected for centuries. The *Yellow Emperor's Canon of Internal Medicine*, which listed 311 diseases, was written around 300 BCE. Metal acupuncture needles were already in use one thousand years before Baogu was born. By Baogu's time, Chinese doctors had written many texts on acupuncture. Doctors tested herbs and remedies for all kinds of illnesses. They noted the results and passed the information on. Some Daoists searched for a pill or potion that would give people eternal life. As they searched, they learned about chemical reactions, smelting metals, and the properties of many plants and minerals.

Was it strange for Baogu to learn medicine? It was unusual. Most doctors were men. But Baogu may have thought it was normal. Daoists believe the universe is balanced between yin and yang. Yin is dark, cool, and female. Yang is light, warm, and male. Male and female balance each other. Daoism has both male and female gods. Baogu must have heard the stories of the powerful Queen Mother of the West who could give life or healing if she chose. Perhaps she believed, as did many early Chinese people, that the Kitchen God, who controlled food, was a woman. Baogu would have seen Daoist nuns passing through the village or helping the poor. There was always a place in the Daoist world for women. Baogu may have believed it was not only right, but her duty to learn medicine from her father.

Baogu was a good student and a good doctor. She became an expert at moxibustion. Moxibustion is a way to treat illness by holding a bundle of burning moxa, the herb mugwort, over certain places on the patient's body. She would have spent a long time try-

---

Laozi

According to legend, Laozi (also spelled Lao Tzu) was the founder of Daoism (Taoism). He is said to have lived sometime between 600 BCE and 400 BCE, possibly at the same time as Confucius. In fact, no one knows for sure if Lao Tzu was a real person. Tradition says he wrote the major text of Daoism, the *Daodejing (Tao Te Ching)*. This text, which may be a collection of wisdom from many teachers, encourages people to seek truth through meditation and simplicity, by overcoming desire, and living in tune with nature. As all things have dual aspects (yin and yang), it emphasizes seeking balance and harmony.

---

ing out her techniques. She and her father probably discussed the difficult cases. She knew the villagers she treated. She must have been pleased to relieve an old woman's pain, or thrilled to save a friend's baby from a fever.

Although Baogu was a Daoist and a doctor, she was also a woman. Chinese people in her time lived with Confucian laws and ideas too. She would be expected to marry. Her family would choose her husband for her. Would he allow her to keep practicing medicine? Would he let her go to the woods by herself to gather herbs? Her family must have thought of this. They solved the problem by marrying her to another doctor.

Together Baogu and her husband, Ge Hong, gathered herbs, tested remedies, and treated many people. They also wrote a book on moxibustion. Baogu became famous for her ability to treat tumors. Old records say she spent her life traveling throughout Guangdong, gathering herbs and healing the sick, honored by all.

Three Traditions

During much of Chinese history, Confucianism, which described social roles and ways of acting, was the official government philosophy. But Chinese people were not bound to one philosophy or religion. Daoism grew out of ancient beliefs and folklore. It included magic, many spirits and gods, a belief that humans could become immortal, and an awareness of nature. Daoists pursued these ideas. Many were doctors, or alchemists, or martial arts experts. Ordinary people used the best from Daoism, Confucianism, and, later, Buddhism in their daily lives. Daoism and Buddhism had special appeal for women.

Daoist Heroine

Nie Yinniang lived during the later Tang dynasty (618–907). She learned to be an expert at martial arts. Popular legends say that she was kidnapped by a Daoist nun. The nun hid Nie Yinniang in the mountains and taught her all she knew about martial arts and magical spells. The nun returned the girl to her family after five years, but cautioned her to use what she had learned for peace. Nie Yinniang had mastered sword fighting and she easily defeated her father, a Tang general, in a match. Nie Yinniang sometimes left her house at night, disappearing into the countryside. Later, evil people would be found dead, under mysterious circumstances.

Princess Wencheng

Marrying for the Empire
Around 620–680
Tang Dynasty 618–907

The palace at Chang'an was full of activity. It all centered on one girl, Princess Wencheng. She was Tang emperor Taizong's beautiful, talented daughter. Her reputation as a cultured beauty had spread across Asia. Emperor Taizong was going to arrange a marriage for her that would help the empire.

Taizong ruled a great city and a great empire. The early Tang dynasty is known for its tolerance of foreigners and foreign ideas. It wasn't unusual to see visitors from across Asia in Chang'an. Delegations representing the rulers of Korea and Central Asia came to learn Chinese ways. The people in the imperial court enjoyed foreign foods and entertainment.

Now groups of dignitaries arrived asking for Princess Wencheng to be married to their kings. A legend says that Emperor Taizong devised an elaborate contest to see who was clever enough to claim Wencheng. The representative from Tibet won. Taizong began arrangements for Wencheng's marriage.

Maybe Princess Wencheng learned about her future husband, King Sron-tsan of Tibet, through gossip. He hadn't come to Chang'an himself, so she could only imagine what he might be like. Perhaps she asked around the court, looking for anyone who had traveled to Tibet. It was far to the west, in the mountains. She may have heard stories of Tibet's snow-covered mountains, fast-moving rivers, or fierce winds.

She also may have heard strange things about the people. Chinese people were not fond of western nomads. For centuries, they had fought them along the borders of the empire. Some nomads dressed in skins, not silk. They buttoned their jackets down the side, not in front as the Chinese did. Nomads were animal herders.

They drank milk and ate butter. Most Chinese were farmers, used to eating grains and vegetables.

Wencheng would have to live in Tibet with nomadic people. She probably didn't think of it as an adventure. Travel wasn't easy. It would take weeks to get there. She might never see her friends and family again. She didn't speak the Tibetan language. How would she even talk to her husband? She may have read the poem, written hundreds of years before, by the Han princess Wusun. Princess Wusun was married to a Turk and sent to live with him. She wrote:

> Oh, my family has married me to the
> first who offered,
> And they left me in this strange and
> distant land,
> Wife to the King of Wusun
> With a domed hut for my boudoir, oh!
> And felt for walls.
> Meat for my dinner, oh!
> And curdled milk to drink.
> To live in this barbarous land
> Wounds me to my soul,
> I long to tread the yellow earth
> And return to my old home.

> **Controlling an Empire**
> Chinese rulers used many methods to gather non-Chinese people into the empire. Some tribes were defeated in war. The leaders of others were bought off, often with silk. Some tribes and kingdoms acknowledged China's power by offering tribute—luxurious gifts and taxes—to the Chinese emperor. In return, the emperor sent lavish gifts to the foreign royalty. And since Han times, emperors had invited sons of foreign leaders to "live and study" in the Chinese capital. These sons were trained in Chinese ways but they were really hostages. If a foreign prince caused trouble, his sons could be punished or killed. But one of the most effective ways to strengthen the empire's power was through royal marriage such as Wencheng's.

Would Wencheng, like Wusun, soon be weeping for China's yellow soil? Although she might have felt scared or worried, she would not have questioned her marriage. When the Emperor Taizong considered winning the loyalty of neighboring tribes, he thought of making them part of the family. If he married his daughters to foreigners—Turks, Mongols, or Tibetans—the women would represent the empire in foreign places. Their new families would be part of the emperor's family. Princess Wencheng knew she was part of a plan to expand the empire. She could not refuse. Her marriage might bring peace and cooperation between the Chinese empire and the kingdom of Tibet.

That doesn't mean she was happy. Maybe she begged her father for the company of the dozens of people who were now preparing to travel to Tibet with her. Or maybe, knowing how lonely she might be, it was his idea to send a bit of China with her. Maybe he intended a show of power and generosity to the Tibetan king. Did Princess Wencheng swear she couldn't live without Chinese musicians to remind her of home? Did her father tell her she must be responsible for the ironworkers and farmers he was sending to Tibet? No one recorded their conversations. But court officials did record details of the group that traveled from Chang'an to Lhasa, Tibet. The emperor provided a library of Chinese books, seeds, silkworms, and medicines. He sent ladies-in-waiting and the craftspeople, physicians, and musicians to go with the supplies. And Princess Wencheng also took an image of Buddha.

Princess Wencheng left Chang'an in 641 CE. The journey took one month. The road was hot, dry, and dusty. Wencheng must have longed for the luxury of the palace. Even twenty-five ladies-in-waiting couldn't take away the dust from her mouth or sooth the fatigue of travel.

Buddhism Began in India
Buddhist ideas were brought to China during the Period of Disunion (220–589 CE). After the Han dynasty collapsed in 220, there were years of war. Powerful lords fought each other for control. They divided and redivided China into regional kingdoms and dynasties. During this 350-year period, power changed often and the change was often bloody. In times of war and uncertainty, more people turned to religion to find salvation from the pain and terror of the crumbling Chinese world. Many Chinese became Buddhists. Buddhism flourished in early Tang China. Chinese women found comfort in Buddhist meditation and prayer. In later centuries, Buddhism continued to be popular with women whose lives were controlled by family and men. Upper-class Song, Ming, or Qing dynasty women, who weren't allowed to leave their homes for everyday reasons, could go to religious services at the temple. Meditating at home gave women moments of peace.

Finally, as the travelers approached Qinghai, they saw a lovely pavilion in the distance. King Sron-tsan had ordered it built for their meeting. The king and many Tibetan officials greeted the travelers. He escorted Princess

Wencheng on to Lhasa, the capital of Tibet. The Tibetan people welcomed her. She must have been happy with her king, because soon she was happy in Tibet.

The craftsmen who traveled with her from China taught Tibetans the Chinese techniques for planting, spinning, weaving, and working with iron. The king became a Buddhist. He had a huge monastery, the Jokhan, built in the center of Lhasa for the image of Buddha that Wencheng had brought from China. Princess Wencheng saw that Tibetans didn't have a written language. She urged the king to have an alphabet created so Tibetans could read and write in their own language. Buddhist texts, Chinese history, and literature were rewritten in the new script. Wencheng and King Sron-tsan's marriage cemented a peace treaty between China and Tibet that lasted twenty years. Today, each April 15, Tibetans celebrate the Sagedawa Festival, to honor the Tang princess who changed Tibet.

Guanyin

Buddhism grew and changed in the tolerant atmosphere of the early Tang. One popular form of Buddhism honored Guanyin, the Goddess of Mercy. Guanyin is a bodhisattva, a person who has agreed to be born on earth over and over again until all souls have a chance to learn and reach nirvana, the Buddhist heaven. In China, Guanyin is a beautiful woman. In India, this bodhisattva is a represented by a man, Avalokitesvara. He was one of two brothers who promised to attend the Buddha. This god, who gives life and helps the troubled, seemed female to the Chinese. They built temples for her, and created statues and art to honor her. Childless women prayed to her, hoping to become pregnant. Even today, she is one of China's best-loved symbols, a special patron of women and children.

Wu Zetian

Emperor of China
625–705
Tang Dynasty 618–907

Maybe the times set the stage for Wu Zetian to become emperor. During the Tang dynasty, upper-class women rode horses, played polo, and went hunting. Chang'an, the Tang capital, was home to many foreigners. They brought their foods, dances, languages, religions, and ideas with them. New things were acceptable in China.

Still, no one imagined a woman would become emperor. The idea would probably have surprised Wu Zetian herself when she was a girl. Wu Zetian was born to a wealthy family who named her Wu Zhao. As a member of a wealthy household, she received education in music and literature. She grew to be stunningly beautiful. Her beauty caught the eye of the emperor, and at age fourteen she was brought to his palace. She became a concubine to the powerful Tang emperor, Taizong (the father of Princess Wencheng). Wu took a new name, Meiniang, Beautiful Girl.

Wu Meiniang soon became Taizong's favorite concubine. But Taizong died, and she was sent to live in a Buddhist monastery. The quiet, simple life of the monastery wasn't what Wu Meiniang wanted. Sweeping floors and carrying firewood at the monastery must have been hard and boring compared to being entertained and waited on at the palace. She must have missed the activity and luxury of the court. She preferred nibbling fresh fruit, bathing in scented water, and gossiping with her palace friends to praying and meditating. When the new emperor, Gaozong, visited her monastery, she knew what she wanted. She charmed him into bringing her back to his court. She became Gaozong's concubine. Soon she was one of his favorites, too.

Life in the emperor's court was easier than life in the monastery, but it must have been terrifying at times. The emperor held the power of life and death over the Chinese people. But he needed the help of others to manage his huge empire. The people who lived in the palace provided aid and advice. They could change the empire. The emperor might reward them with extravagant gifts, lands, or titles. But he also might get angry with them and have them put to death. Wu Meiniang, like the others at the court, needed to please the emperor and have the right friends in order to survive.

Wives and concubines competed for the emperor's attention. Ministers and officials tried to keep their power and position by helping friends and family, and getting rid of enemies. Jealousy, schemes, intrigue, and deception were all part of day-to-day palace life. Wu Meiniang made friends with other people at the palace. Friends could share gossip and news. Perhaps it was a servant who told Wu Meiniang that Emperor Gaozong's wife was so jealous of Wu Meiniang that she was plotting to kill her.

Wu Meiniang made her own plan. Wu Meiniang had just given birth to the emperor's baby daughter. She smothered the baby, and then blamed the emperor's wife for the murder. Her plan worked. Emperor Gaozong sent his wife away and married Wu Meiniang. Now she was the empress of China. She took a new name, Wu Zetian.

In 660, Emperor Gaozong had a stroke. He was unable to rule as he had before. This was not the first time an emperor was too sick to carry out his duties. A few empresses in the past had ruled "behind the screen." They acted for weak, young sons or old, sick husbands. In Confucian China, it was a man's place to rule. Even an empress would not be present at meetings of high officials. So empresses who needed information sat hidden behind a screen. They passed information and their recommendations to their ailing

---

Concubines

Emperors, officials, and other rich men often had many wives. A man's first, official wife was respected as her husband's mate and had recognized rights and duties. When a man took a wife, he made an official connection with her family. Her sons might inherit his lands and money. His other women were concubines. They had a lower position in the household. Concubines were often beautiful or talented women who interested wealthy men. They kept the men company and might have their children. But they had to be careful. Concubines had no rights in the household and could be sent away at any time.

husbands. Often, they made decisions themselves without consulting their husbands. With Gaozong unable to rule, Wu Zetian took her place behind the screen.

Wu Zetian knew what was expected of court women. She understood how Confucian tradition kept women from holding true power. Only the emperor or other male officials performed important Confucian ceremonies. She decided to publicly challenge tradition. In 666, she led a group of women to Mt. Tai (Taishan), in Shandong, one of China's sacred mountains. Emperors often went there to pray. Now it was Wu Zetian who conducted the holy rites.

And in 673, while Emperor Gaozong was still alive, Wu Zetian paid twenty thousand copper *cash* (a type of money) to have artists carve a fifty-six-foot-tall statue of the Buddha of the Future for the emperor's own temple at the Longmen Grottos. This was a major Buddhist shrine near Luoyang, Henan. Legend says this Buddha's face looks just like Empress Wu's. She claimed a Buddhist text predicted a "Sage Mother" would rule China. The "Sage (wise) Mother", who happened to look like her, would direct years of happiness and plenty. Next, Wu Zetian built Buddhist temples dedicated to the Sage Mother.

Wu Zetian continued to create her own power. She directed the empire's scholars to write biographies of famous women. Drawing attention to other important Chinese women strengthened her position with the scholars, who traditionally gave their blessings to China's rulers.

Courtesans
Gongsun Daniang (700–762) was a courtesan and dancer. Wealthy, educated men wanted to spend time with talented women. Courtesans were women who had been trained as dancers, singers, poets, or keen thinkers. Through much of Chinese history, courtesans, like concubines, were among the few women who might gain power over the men who admired them. They might also gain freedom from women's usual responsibilities. Gongsun Daniang was famous for dancing the *jianqi*, or sword dance. At age seventeen, she was chosen to join the emperor's palace dancers. She performed for the court and traveled the empire, dazzling crowds with her dancing and flashing swords. Tang poet Du Fu saw Gongsun dance when he was a child. Fifty years later, he wrote a poem about her. Calligraphy master Xiang Zu saw Gongsun dance too. Afterwards, it is said, his style was freer and had more movement, like the famous dancer.

When Gaozong died in 683, Wu Zetian had been making decisions about the empire for twenty-three years. She didn't want to stop. After he died, she made sure the imperial throne went to a weak heir, Gaozong's son Zhongzong. He ruled for only six weeks before Wu Zetian accused him of treason and replaced him with his younger brother Ruizong. Although Ruizong was emperor for four years, Wu Zetian was the true ruler of China.

In 690, Ruizong formally gave up his title. Wu Zetian declared herself Emperor of China. She chose strong ministers to help her rule. One was a woman, Shangguan Wan'er, whose duties were like those of a prime minister. Shangguan Wan'er's father and grandfather had both been executed for opposing Empress Wu. But Shangguan Wan'er herself was a devoted scribe, advisor, and spy in Wu Zetian's court. She became powerful and served the court even after Wu Zetian's death.

Wu Zetian held the title of emperor for only fifteen years but she was the real ruler of China for almost fifty years, from 660 to her death in 705. She built her power through beauty, intelligence, intrigue, and force. She put her skills to work for China. Under her rule, the Tang empire expanded. She saved the empire money by having soldiers grow their own food when they weren't fighting. She supported irrigation projects that helped farmers. She allowed common people to bring their problems to her. As the text of the "Sage Mother" predicted, Wu Zetian, who started her court life as a favored concubine, became an emperor who ruled over a time of peace and plenty in China.

Scholars and the Mandate of Heaven

Scholars were often the people who interpreted the ruler's actions to others, and rulers needed their support. Scholars studied ancient history and values. They could say whether or not a ruler was pleasing to Heaven. The "Mandate of Heaven" was an idea that took root in Han times. It said that the emperor was a part of the Heaven and the Earth, something like the way a conductor is part of a symphony orchestra. If the emperor's actions were good, the empire prospered. If the actions were bad, terrible things could happen. Comets might appear in the sky. Earthquakes or floods could cause death and destruction. Then scholars and other people might say Heaven was unhappy with the emperor. An emperor who lost the "Mandate of Heaven" might soon be facing a revolt!

Many stories of Wu Zetian's life emphasize her cruel actions toward her rivals. Most of these accounts were written in later centuries by male historians. These men served male emperors who probably felt a woman should never have ruled China. Today's historians must consider how much of what was recorded is true, and how much was included to damage the memory of the woman empress.

The Story of Luofu

Wu Zetian was not the first beautiful woman brought to the emperor's court to become a concubine. Some girls were offered by their families, others were taken against their will. There are many stories about these women. While some tell of women who accepted their fate or were unable to do anything to change it, others honor women who resisted their captors. This one is one about Luofu who lived hundreds of years before Wu Zetian, during the Han dynasty.

Luofu was a beautiful teenage girl who worked raising silkworms and weaving silk. One day Luofu was gathering mulberry leaves for her silk worms. A high official passed her in his carriage. He stopped and spoke to her. The official invited Luofu to get in his carriage and come for a ride with him. But she knew he probably wanted more than just an afternoon ride. She also knew that standing up to a court official could be very dangerous. Any girl would be afraid to refuse a governor what he wanted. She or her family could be punished. But not Luofu.

Luofu called the governor a fool. She said he was probably married and that she had a husband. She stood defiantly, waiting for his reply. But instead of taking her forcibly or punishing her, the official galloped away when Luofu was brave enough to tell the truth.

Li Qingzhao

Poet and Wife
1084–1151
Song Dynasty 960–1279

Li Qingzhao lived in wartime. During the Song dynasty the Chinese empire was shrinking at the same time that Chinese culture was flourishing. The earlier Tang empire had grown so large that by 907 the emperor couldn't control all his generals and officials. The empire broke into separate areas. Each was ruled by a strong official and each fought for power over its neighbors. The Chinese emperor was left with only a small piece of the old empire around the capital.

Smaller non-Chinese empires and kingdoms grew up in the north and west of the old Tang empire. The Chinese didn't command the respect and tribute of most of East Asia anymore. Their armies weren't the most powerful. Foreigners no longer jammed the capital city. The Chinese turned inward to their traditional culture and education as a source of pride.

Changes in society and in attitudes affected Li Qingzhao and other Song dynasty women's lives. Upper-class girls growing up in Shangdong Province could not expect to hunt or ride as girls had during the Tang. Song China was much more urban. Even rich landowners lived in cities. Song women led quiet lives.

During the Song dynasty, it became common for upper-class women to live most of their lives in rooms separate from men in their own homes. Li Qingzhao would have grown up in the women's quarters. Upper-class houses were large, often built around a rectangular courtyard. Each side of the house had its own purpose. The front of the house had public rooms for receiving guests. There was a place for honoring ancestors and a study for the men. Women and their children lived in special quarters in the back of the courtyard. Women did not meet with men who weren't members of their families. Husbands visited their wives and children in the women's quarters, but women came to the public, front parts of the house only for family ceremonies and to honor ancestors. They rarely, if ever, went outside the house and its courtyard.

As a little girl, Li Qingzhao probably played in the women's quarters. She might have watched fish swim in a pool in the courtyard. Perhaps she had a favorite kitten or chickens she cared for. She might have had a servant to help her dress. Her mother probably taught her to weave and sew. But she would only have peeked down from the roof or window at poorer girls who were allowed to go out in the village.

Wives and daughters of commoners were not confined to their homes. In towns, they worked in shops or side by side with their husbands. Some kept accounts, made bargains, or served customers. Lower-class women, not rich women, enjoyed the jugglers and storytellers in the crowded city markets. They were the ones who could trade a coin for a mooncake or a peach from a farmer's stall. Some were matchmakers, or entertainers who mixed with powerful men from fine families. Others were servants or slave girls who ran errands for their masters.

While men and commoner women passed by outside, upper-class women worked in their quarters. A woman whose husband was an imperial official stationed far away might run the family's farms and businesses. She would meet tenants and business associates in the courtyard of the women's quarters.

Many upper-class women were weavers. Chinese people had always paid taxes in grain, strings of copper called *cash,* and cloth. Women wove the cloth. In Li Qingzhao's house, as in Song households across China, women wove silk and hemp in their quarters. Weaving was women's work.

Women also embroidered and made beautiful needlework for their daughter's dowries. A dowry was what a girl's family sent with her to her husband's home when she married. It could include money, silk and cotton fabric, needlework, clothing, personal items, and perhaps land. A good dowry made a girl a desirable wife. The dowry was the only property a woman, such as Li Qingzhao's mother, owned. She kept it in her rooms and could use it to help herself and her children. She could sell part of her dowry if she needed money, or use it for gifts to other members of her new household. A fine dowry could make a bride's life easier after she left her parents' home.

Li Qingzhao and her mother probably spent hours weaving cloth for her dowry. One thing that Li Qingzhao could count on was that she would marry. Almost all Chinese girls did. But, for Li Qingzhao, marriage presented a special problem. Song scholars suggested that upper-class families teach their daughters to read, write, and study texts, such as *Biographies of Famous Women* and Ban Zhao's *Lessons for Women*. Li Qingzhao's parents were both writers. They had taught her to read and write. She loved words and poetry, even as a young girl. Would a husband keep her from her studies and from writing poetry? Would he share her love of language? Who would her parents choose for her? Would his parents treat her well? Li Qingzhao must have had a thousand questions.

Marriage, for most medieval Chinese girls, was not exciting and romantic. It was a time of uncertainty and probably fear. Still, ending up as a wife was better than being sold. Poor girls, whose families could not feed them, were often sold as servants, concubines, or entertainers. They were like slaves in their new household. An ordinary girl could hope for marriage to a family like her own.

> **Silk Weaving**
> Records from the Han dynasty say a woman could weave two and one half to five feet of silk cloth in a day. She needed more than a week to weave a bolt, forty feet. Silk fabric was used as money. During the Han dynasty, forty feet of silk weighed one Chinese pound, worth 512 copper *cash*, a type of money. In Song times (960–1279), a family of ten could raise the silkworms, spin and weave the silk for thirty-one bolts of silk in a year. Those thirty-one bolts would sell for enough money to feed the family for the year.

Li Qingzhao's family would choose her husband, and once she married she would move to her husband's family's house. Chinese families used marriage to strengthen their own families. They looked for a husband whose family could provide for their daughter, and for a strong wife with a good dowry for their sons. Upper-class Chinese families, such as Li Qingzhao's, also tried to unite with other powerful families. They looked for grooms whose families could help them in business and in dealing with the government, and who could bring them respect in the community. Few upper-class Chinese would waste an opportunity to use their daughter's marriage to make a good connection. Parents of girls like Li Qingzhao would not allow a daughter to marry below the family's position.

Marriage

When a Song dynasty upper-class girl was old enough to marry, her parents contacted a matchmaker. The matchmaker knew of families looking for wives for their sons. She told the girl's parents how hardworking, intelligent, or rich a certain boy was. She explained how a groom's family could help them in business, in dealing with officials, or in times of war or famine. Boys' families wanted to find a girl who would fit into their household. Would she know how to care for her in-laws and husband? Would she be able to give birth to healthy children, especially sons? Did she come from a family that could help theirs? If the families agreed their children would marry, the groom's family paid a bride price of money and gifts. The bride's family promised a dowry. On the wedding day, a special procession of the groom and his friends went to the bride's home. The bride walked through her parent's gates, leaving her childhood family behind. At the groom's home, his family waited to greet her. She was presented to his parents, relatives, and in a special ceremony, to his dead ancestors. More ceremonies and feasting ended with the couple going to their rooms in the women's quarters for the night. Her new life had begun.

But there are many examples of parents who thought of their daughter's future happiness too. Li Qingzhao's parents did. They chose another scholar, Zhao Mingcheng, for her husband. He would support her love of writing.

Li Qingzhao became a famous poet. Her work was admired by other poets. But many Chinese people still thought women shouldn't write poetry. One woman turned down Li's offer to teach her, saying writing poetry wasn't a proper thing for women to do.

Li and her husband were successful upper-class Song scholars who lived happy and comfortable lives. Through the years, they collected many antiques, rare books, and paintings. Li Qingzhao's poems were often about love, fun, and happiness. But during the Song dynasty, China was frequently at war with its neighbors. When Jin (Mongol) armies invaded, everyone was in danger. In 1127, Jin and Song soldiers battled for control of northern China. As the fighting got closer to their home, Li Qingzhao and her husband packed ten carts of precious books and antiques and fled.

They joined a line of refugees who headed south, away from the Jin soldiers. Old people and babies, pampered women and hard-working servants, farmers with their oxen and chickens, all filled the roads to the south. Eventually, the emperor and his court fled south too. Northern China fell to the Mongolian Jin.

Less than two years after fleeing the north, Li Qingzhao's husband died. She had lost most of their precious collection as she struggled to get to southern China. Although she was uprooted and lonely, she continued to write. Many of her poems now showed her despair with the Song government. She urged it to fight the Jin and recapture northern China.

> *Lonely in my secluded chamber,*
> *A thousand sorrows fill every inch*
>   *of my sensitive being.*
> *Regretting that spring has so soon passed,*
> *That rain drops have hastened the falling flowers,*
> *I lean over the balustrade,*
> *Weary and depressed.*
> *Where is my beloved?*
> *Only the fading grassland*
>   *stretches endlessly toward the horizon;*
> *Anxiously I watch the road for your return.*

Huang Daopo

Famous Weaver
1245–1300
Yuan Dynasty 1279–1368

When Huang Daopo was a girl, she may not have even known that northern China was no longer ruled by Chinese people. The Mongols had conquered the north and during her lifetime they would come to govern all of China. But that probably didn't matter much to Huang Daopo. She was a little Chinese girl living in Songjiang County, near today's Shanghai. Most families she knew were poor like hers. They had bigger problems than worrying about who ruled China. Huang Daopo went to bed hungry on many nights.

Poor or not, families had to pay taxes to the government in grain or bolts of cloth. When women could be spared from working in the fields, they wove. Farming families divided their work. Men and women, old people and children, had different jobs. Men did the plowing and planting. Women raised silkworms, spun the silk into thread, and wove cloth. Girls like Huang Daopo began to learn this work when they were young children.

But Huang Daopo's family needed more than a girl who could weave. It cost a lot to raise a child. And just as a daughter was old enough to really work and benefit the family, she would be married and move in with her in-laws. So, Huang Daopo's parents did what many poor people did. When Huang Daopo was still very young, her family sold her to another family to be a future wife for their son. She moved into the home of her future husband. He might have been a child himself. He might have been much older. We don't know. It only mattered that his family had more money than hers. Huang Daopo's family got money they needed. They no longer had the expense of raising her. This helped their whole family survive. But it probably felt horrible to Huang Daopo. Perhaps she would have starved if she stayed with her family. But she must have been scared to leave her mother and the home she knew.

She would have known only her family and a few friends in her village. Now she was moving into a new household where she didn't know anyone. She would not go as an honored bride. She wasn't old enough. She would have to earn her keep until she was old enough to marry and have grandchildren for her in-laws. Child brides were expected to carry water, sew, weave, scrub, and cook. Huang Daopo became her future in-law's servant.

Probably other people in the household reminded her that she was poor and told her how lucky she was to have food to eat and a place to sleep. They would have taught her to obey her future husband, no matter what his age. Huang Daopo's new family beat her when they weren't happy with her work. She must have felt desperately lonely and angry. She made a plan to escape. A fainthearted girl wouldn't have run away. If she were caught, she'd be punished. In Confucian China, a man could punish his family's servant girl as he chose. She must have known she could be beaten, sold, or even killed. Still she went ahead with her plan.

Huang Daopo found a ship anchored in the nearby river. She hid in the boat until it sailed. She might not have known or cared where it was going. Eventually the boat landed south of China at Hainan Island, and Huang Daopo stepped into a strange place. She was free of her family, but what would she do?

The people of Hainan Island weren't Han Chinese. They were Li people. They spoke a different language and had different ways of doing things. Did

---

The Silk Trade

The Yuan rulers of China, who reigned during Huang Daopo's lifetime, were Mongol people from the north. Their empire reached across Asia to Europe. Ever since the Han dynasty, traders had carried silk, woven by Chinese women, along the Silk Road to the Middle East and Europe. The Silk Road trade was especially good during the Yuan dynasty. The Mongol rulers of China controlled most of Central Asia, too, making it easier for caravans to travel across Asia. Lines of camels pushed west from Chang'an, loaded with porcelain, lacquerware, and the silk produced by Chinese women. Silk might be headed for a tribal leader in Samarkind or a trader on the Mediterranean Sea. It was valued across two continents. Traders could make small fortunes from silk.

one of the Li families pity the poor girl from China and take her in? Did she live in the countryside outside Li villages, stealing food until she learned the Li language? Did she hire herself as a servant? We don't know the details. One way or another, Huang Daopo survived. She probably made her living weaving.

When Huang Daopo arrived at Hainan Island, she was amazed at the bright, beautiful cotton cloth the Li people made. Li people didn't raise silkworms and weave silk. For centuries they had grown cotton. They were experts at producing cotton cloth. No one in Songjiang knew the special techniques used by Li people to remove seeds from cotton bolls, or to spin the fibers into thread. Huang Daopo learned everything she could about weaving cotton

Silk had made the Chinese empire wealthy. Silk was traded across the Silk Road from Chang'an to Europe. Camel drivers, traders, and officials all made money from silk. But the women weavers in Songjiang and

Holeus

Unlike the Chinese, Mongols didn't farm. They herded sheep, horses, and goats. Nomadic Mongol girls learned to ride horses when they were small. They were excellent riders and learned to fight alongside the men. When men were gone, hunting or fighting, women managed their families and herds. They could, by themselves, keep the community fed and clothed.

Holeus was a Mongol woman, the wife of Yesugei. He was the leader of Borijin Mongol tribe. Yesugei was poisoned by a rival and died, leaving their oldest son, Temujin, next in line for power. But the tribe's people were afraid to be led by a young boy. They crept away in the middle of the night and abandoned Holeus and her family.

Left on their own to survive, Holeus demanded that her children learn to work together. Legend says she gave each boy an arrow and told him to break it. The arrows broke easily. Then she took five arrows and tied them together. "Now break the arrows," she said. The boys tried over and over to break the bundle of arrows, but they could not. She said, "We are like arrows. Each one breaks easily, but together we are strong. You must always work together." Eventually, Holeus' son, Temujin, did become the leader of the Borijin tribe. He was called Chinggis Khan (Ghengis Khan). He united the Mongols and led them to conquer most of Asia. Later, Chinggis Khan's daughter-in-law, Sorghaghani Beki, guided her own three sons to power. She was a Nestorian Christian. She taught her sons to be tolerant of religious differences and to support and help peasants. In 1279, her son, Kublai defeated the Song Chinese and became emperor of China. He called his new dynasty the Yuan.

other parts of China didn't get rich. They gave most of the cloth to officials for their taxes. Silk bought the loyalty of some nomad groups and it paid for luxuries in the emperor's court. But it hadn't made Huang Daopo's life easier. Cotton might be different. Huang Daopo saw that cotton might help some poor women in China.

Huang Daopo lived with the Li people for thirty years. She became an expert at weaving cotton cloth. Then, she returned to China. She must have been excited to see her home province again. She may have found her old friends. She was carrying a gift to them. She brought high-quality cotton seeds from Hainan Island. She also brought the tools she needed to spin and weave cotton.

Huang Daopo taught local farmers to raise cotton. She gave them seeds. She taught poor women in her province to dye the cotton fiber in bold colors. And she improved the tools they used to prepare cotton fiber—the cotton gin, bow, and multi-threaded spinning wheel. Soon, women in Songjiang were producing fine cotton cloth. The cloth sold well and families prospered. Maybe Huang Daopo hoped the money from selling cotton would help some little girls stay with their families until they were old enough to marry. Surely, she was proud of being able to help the people in her childhood home.

The Songjiang area is still famous for its fine cotton. Today, Huang Daopo is remembered as China's first cotton expert.

Zhinu and Niulang,
The Cowherd and the Weaver

Huang Daopo was not the first woman to be honored for spinning and weaving skills. Chinese women had been responsible for producing silk for thousands of years. While men tilled fields, women wove. Silk and weaving were so important in China that there are many legends about both. This one is tied to the stars Vega and Altair, and the Milky Way.

Zhinu began her life in heaven. She was the emperor's daughter. But she longed to live among the people on earth. She knew that her father would never allow her to live with common people, so she secretly slipped out of heaven.

Once she was on earth, it wasn't long before she fell in love with a hardworking cowherd, Niulang, and they married. Zhinu was a good wife. And because of her heavenly origins she could spin silk that sparkled like the sky. The couple lived a happy life.

But Zhinu's father, the Emperor of heaven, discovered where she was, and sent soldiers to earth to capture her and return her to her place in the sky. The lovers were separated. Niulang was miserable without his wife and wanted to bring her home. But he was a man, not a celestial being. He couldn't follow her to heaven. So he begged a magic ox to take him. Even this plan didn't work. When Niulang got to Heaven a river of stars kept him from reaching Zhinu.

Close, but not yet together, the lovers turned into stars. He is the star Altair and she is the star Vega. The Milky Way is the river between them. But the legend continues, saying that the Queen Mother of the West felt sorry for the couple. She asked the Emperor of Heaven to let them be together. He agreed, but only for one night each year. So on the seventh night of the seventh lunar month (it falls in August or September), when the stars Vega and Altair are closest to each other, magpies fly to heaven and build a bridge of twigs for the lovers. Zhinu and Niulang cross the bridge and fall into each other's arms.

This night is celebrated in China as the Qi Xi Festival, or Double Seven Festival. It is a night when girls used to offer sacrifices hoping, like Zhinu, to become better at needlework, embroidery, and weaving. These skills would have made girls more desirable as wives, so weaving and falling in love were connected. Double Seven is still celebrated, but today, young lovers are probably less interested in weaving. In China's cities, Double Seven has become like Valentine's Day. Boy friends and girl friends send each other cards or flowers on the night of the Double Seven festival.

Woman Liu, Lady Guan, and Empress Ma

Honored Ming Women
Ming Dynasty 1368–1644

In 1368, Chinese people defeated their Mongol rulers, and established a new, and very Chinese, dynasty, the Ming. After years of living under Mongolian rules and rulers, the new Ming emperors zealously made and enforced Chinese rules. Laws were strict. Upper-class children grew up learning their roles in the ideal Confucian family. Women would marry, care for their families, weave cloth, or perhaps embroider or write poetry. If her husband died, the ideal woman did not remarry.

At the same time, China's population was growing and business was good. Market towns bustled with activity. Small workshops now produced cloth and other goods previously made at home. For the first time, men worked as weavers in weaving shops. Merchants and traders grew wealthy trading along the coast, or between provinces. Southern China was especially prosperous. Bridges arched across the rivers. Walled towns bloomed with gardens. Neat farms produced fruit, vegetables, and rice. Ming emperors sent fleets of huge junks (sailing ships) on expeditions to the South Pacific, India, and Africa.

Ming families admired upper-class traditions. Now many families could afford to copy them. Most families tried to seclude their women, as did the upper class. Even poor girls might live in houses divided by a curtain into men's and women's halves. Many more families began to bind their daughter's feet to keep them tiny and "beautiful."

But, in the thriving Ming cities, there were also more ways for women to live outside traditional roles. Some Ming women made their living as herbalists, midwives, entertainers, or matchmakers. People could afford to pay for their services. Other women, perhaps searching for an ideal life, went off to the mountains to paint, write, or meditate.

Footbinding

Footbinding is said to have begun in the Tang dynasty, when people wanted to imitate a court dancer who was admired for her tiny feet. During the Song dynasty, footbinding became popular with upper-class families. By the end of the Ming dynasty, even some peasant women had bound feet. When a girl was about five years old, her mother tied strips of cloth around her feet and tightened them each night. The strips pulled the four small toes under, against the bottom of her feet. The extremely painful process lasted several years. As the girl grew, her bound feet stayed small. The girl's mother and grandmother probably had bound feet too. They knew how much it hurt and tried to comfort her.

Why would they do this to a child? A girl with tiny feet was considered beautiful. Her feet were compared to lotus blossoms. Parents might not be able to arrange a marriage for a daughter whose feet were not bound. They did it for her future. But the cost, for women, was high. Footbinding crippled women, and kept them close to home. It was difficult for women with bound feet to walk. Peasant girls with bound feet did not work in fields or walk long distances. The practice of footbinding did not end until the twentieth century.

Ming people passed on stories of women who were almost larger than life. Some stories represented the strictest Confucian ideals, while others told of women who did everything except what was expected of them.

The story of Woman Liu begins with magic. When she was a child, bandits attacked her family. No matter how many times the bandits stabbed Woman Liu, they were unable to hurt her. She grew up to study Daoism. According to legend, she found a secret text that said that gods and demons would help Chinese peasant armies who were rebelling against the Yuan Mongol rulers.

As Woman Liu traveled in the mountains, she was able to call on thunderstorms, animals, and earthquakes to help the peasant armies. Her grandfather, a Yuan official, wanted to help the Yuan stay in power. Woman Liu told him that the Mandate of Heaven was passing from the Yuan. He believed her. In 1368 the rebel army defeated the Yuan rulers, and established their own dynasty, the Ming. The new Ming emperor, Zhu Yuanzhang, called Woman Liu to live at the imperial palace. He gave her the title Matron of Subtle Divinity. The emperor could claim he had the right to rule China. Woman Liu had predicted it, and now she was an advisor in his court.

The story of Lady Guan was about everyday duty. Lady Guan was born into a scholar's family in 1483. As a child, she was taught to read and to recite the writings of Confucius. She played with her brothers and sisters, studied her lessons, and learned to embroider. During Ming times, little girls demonstrated their patience and good breeding with fine stitches and detailed designs. In addition to training her to sew and read, Lady Guan's mother would have bound her feet to prepare her for marriage.

She was married when she was fifteen. Her mother-in-law was hard to please, but Lady Guan knew how to make her laugh. She waited on her. She probably fixed her favorite meals, delicate soups, and fragrant teas. She cared for the older woman when she was sick. A few years later Lady Guan's mother-in-law lay dying. She blessed Lady Guan, saying, "May your children and grandchildren achieve great honors."

> **Widows**
> In Ming times, just as in Mengmu's day, a woman's place in the family depended on her husband. When her husband died, his family might arrange for a young widow to remarry. Maybe they would keep her in their household to raise her sons. But they might throw her out. If she couldn't return to her parents' home, she could starve. If she had a dowry to sell she might survive.

When Lady Guan was twenty-one, her husband traveled to Guangdong to care for his aging father. But her husband became ill and died before he could return home. Now, she was a widow with two young children. The ideal Ming woman was expected to remain faithful to her dead husband. But, it wasn't an easy thing to do.

Lady Guan sold the jewels from her dowry so she could pay to bring her husband's body home. She gave him a proper burial. Then she turned to raising her sons. She may have felt it was unfair that she was supposed to live out her life alone. But she never complained about the hard days of caring for her family.

Through the years, Lady Guan carefully tutored and encouraged her sons. One son grew up to become an official and a teacher. She was kind and generous to the poor, and always had small gifts for the women she met.

Lady Guan lived the life of the virtuous widow who remained faithful to her husband's family and ancestors even after his death.

This idea was so important to the Ming government that at one time it honored faithful widows with special stone arches outside their homes. Widows were living examples of morality, and morality gave Ming China its authority.

While Woman Liu had spiritual power and Lady Guan had moral power, Lin Mo was revered for her strength and ability to save lives. Lin Mo (960–987) lived on the seacoast of Fujian Province during the earlier Tang dynasty. During the Ming dynasty her story became a favorite of traveling merchants and sailors.

Lin was a great swimmer. She often rowed out to sea, risking her life to rescue drowning people. Then she met her final challenge. There was a huge storm. One after another, she saved nine people from a sinking merchant ship. Swimming hard against the waves, she struggled to reach another desperate sailor. But, legend says, she drowned, and a red carriage carried her spirit to heaven. Lin Mo became a goddess—Empress Ma (Mazu), or Goddess of Heaven. From her place in heaven, she protected sailors and rescued sinking ships. During the Ming dynasty, Chinese sailors carried the story of Empress Ma wherever they went. Many temples were built to honor her in Fujian and on the southern islands. In later centuries, as Chinese people emigrated to South Asia and beyond, Empress Ma watched over them. Empress Ma, the strong protector whose story captured the Ming imagination, outlived the dynasty. Even today, she is honored, especially in Taiwan.

Temples to Empress Ma

Temples to Lin Mo, Goddess of Heaven and the Sea, have been built in many countries. San Francisco, California, has two. The Tin How Temple, the oldest, was built by Chinese who arrived during the 1849 Gold Rush. People still climb its narrow stairway to light incense, make offerings, or leave red cards asking for help from the goddess.

Nushu: Women's Writing

In medieval China, women were rarely taught to read and write. But women in Hunan Province created their own system of writing. It may have its roots as early as 300 CE and quite likely was in use by the Ming dynasty. Mothers taught daughters and friends taught friends. It is called *nushu* or women's writing. It was not taught to men. The women embroidered nushu messages on cloth or painted it on fans which they exchanged. Nushu allowed the women to express their feelings.

Girls in that part of Hunan were often matched as children with girls from other villages. They became special friends called *laotong*. Their families approved of the friendship, much as they would approve of a marriage. The girls sealed the arrangement by sending each other fans with good wishes and pledges of friendship written in nushu. The girls visited each other and became close to each other's families. They spent time doing needlework and talking together. Sometimes girls from the same village would form a sisterhood. Writing in nushu, they invited up to seven girls to join their club. The "sisters" met often and visited together.

When a laotong or member of a sisterhood married and moved to her new husband's family and village, her special friends sent her messages in nushu. They said how sad they were to see her marry and move away and how difficult it would be to live without her. As the girls married, they often lost touch with each other.

Today, Chinese girls don't need to learn nushu. They go to school and learn to read and write Chinese characters and pinyin. Although there are many examples of nushu from the late Qing dynasty and early twentieth century, there are few people left who can read and write it. Yang Huanyi, probably the last elderly women to use nushu, died in 2004 but scholars are trying to preserve the writing.

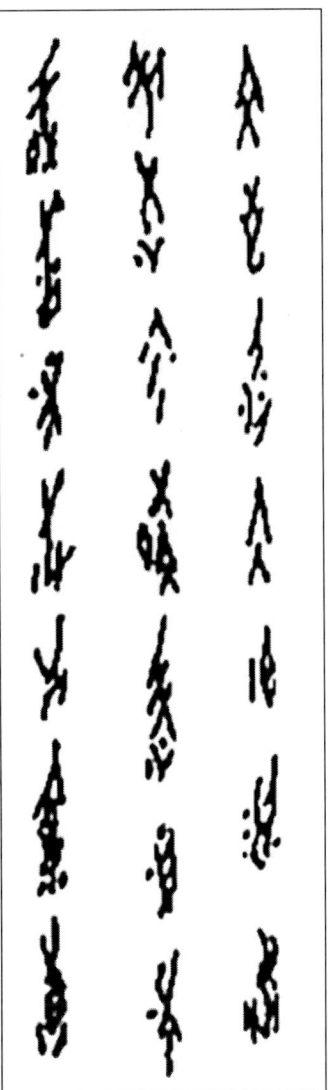

Some people compare nushu's strokes to long embroidery stitches.

Zhen Yuanyuan

A Beautiful Pawn
1623–1685
Ming Dynasty 1368–1644

Zhen Yuanyuan was born to a poor family. When she was still a child her family sold her, and she was taken to Suzhou to learn to entertain men for money. Many poor girls who were sold to be entertainers, servants, or laborers were used and soon forgotten. However, Zhen Yuanyuan's life turned out differently. Although she didn't plan it, powerful officials would pursue her, and a general would betray his country for her.

When Zhen Yuanyuan's family sold her, she was probably afraid she'd be beaten or abused. That didn't happen. The person who bought her loved her and trained her with kindness. At seventeen, Yuanyuan began singing, dancing, and entertaining men. She was beautiful and charming. One after another, men fell under her spell and she became famous throughout China. She must have loved her power over men who waited to talk to her or to have a moment alone with her. She may have felt she would always be the center of a charmed world where her beauty gave her some control over others.

But everything changed when Dian Wan, a high official, stole Zhen Yuanyuan and set out to take her to the capital, Beijing. He planned to use her to get ahead. She must have been terrified. Perhaps she tried to escape. Did she know where she was going? Or what Dian Wan was about to do?

Her captor took her to the palace and offered her to the Ming emperor, but the emperor wasn't interested and refused the gift. Dian Wan didn't give up. He thought of another plan to use the beautiful Zhen Yuanyuan. He introduced her to Wu Sangui, a powerful Ming general, hoping to gain favors from him later on. This plan worked. Wu Sangui and Zhen Yuanyuan fell in love.

But the Ming dynasty, weakened by corruption, bad management, droughts and famines, was in trouble. Wu Sangui had to go to

The Imperial Palace and Imperial City

The Imperial Palace (Forbidden City) was the center of the Chinese empire during the Ming and Qing dynasties. The Ming emperor Yongle ordered its construction. Workers began building its grand halls, temples, residences, and gardens in 1406. It became the seat of China's government and home to the emperor and his court. When it was completed, the Imperial Palace had more than nine thousand individual rooms. The grounds covered about a square mile. Walls more than thirty feet high surrounded the city. Visitors entered through impressive gateways. Ordinary people were not allowed into the Imperial Palace unless they were on official business. Women who entered as wives or concubines might spend their entire lives without leaving its grounds again.

Next to the Imperial Palace was an area called Imperial City, three square miles of workshops and warehouses. More than one hundred thousand people worked in Imperial City to keep the emperor's household running. South of the Imperial Palace was the Outer City where common people lived. Modern Beijing grew up around this imperial complex.

Today, more than twelve million people live in Beijing. The Imperial Palace is now the Palace Museum (Gu Gong, Former Palace), open to everyone.

war. The Manchus had invaded China, even crossing the Great Wall before being beaten back. And, once again, a large army of angry peasants was in revolt. In 1644, with the peasant army at the outskirts of the capital city, the Ming emperor committed suicide.

Now the peasants and the Manchus battled each other. The winner would rule China. Wu Sangui still controlled a powerful army. Both the Manchus and the peasants wanted him to leave the Ming army and fight for them. Each group hoped to capture Zhen Yuanyuan and use her as a hostage to gain the general's help. But Zhen Yuanyuan had fled her home. According to one story, the leader of the peasant army tortured Wu Sangui's father, trying to find out where she was hiding. Wu Sangui was angry and decided to fight for the Manchus. He led his great army south. This time he was fighting for the Manchus instead of the Ming. Zhen Yuanyuan traveled with Wu Sangui as his army pursued the remaining Ming troops. It must not have been easy to travel with the army. This life was far different from life entertaining admiring men in a quiet garden. Some days there might not have been enough food. Ming troops could always attack them. But it may have seemed safer to Zhen Yuanyuan to travel with Wu Sangui than to wait at home alone.

As a reward for his service to the Manchus, Wu Sangui was appointed governor of Yunnan Province. Later, he declared himself emperor of his own separate dynasty. Now Manchu forces attacked him again. When he was defeated, legend says Zhen Yuanyuan lost all hope. One story says she became a Buddhist nun, and later hanged herself. Another says she threw herself into a lake and drowned.

The Manchu

In the early 1600s, Jurchen tribes from Manchuria began to attack the Ming government. By the 1640s, and now calling themselves "Manchu," they were a powerful force that had repeatedly crossed the Great Wall to battle Ming armies. The Chinese peasant army that conquered Beijing in 1644 and ended the Ming dynasty was not able to hold on to power. In less than a year it was defeated by the Manchu, aided by former Ming armies. The Manchu named their dynasty Qing. Eventually, after years of fighting, they controlled south China too. There were over one hundred million Chinese to control. But there were only a few million Manchu. The Manchu adopted Han customs, traditional Chinese ways, and conservative Confucian philosophy to gain the support of China's scholars and the upper class. They used Chinese, Mongol, and Manchu people in their government and ruled China in a very Chinese style.

Hong Xuanjiao

Taiping Warrior
About 1820–1864
Qing Dynasty 1644–1912

Hong Xuanjiao was a Hakka woman. Although Hakka people were Chinese, they had a different culture from their neighbors. Hakka men and women worked together. Men often took jobs in towns, leaving the women to tend children and fields. Hakka women didn't bind their feet. They were partners in supporting their families. They planted and weeded gardens. They walked miles along steep paths in the mountains of Guangdong, Guangxi, Hunan, Jiangxi, and Fujian where most Hakkas lived. Hakka women were strong and forthright. It wasn't surprising that they would join men in a revolution.

By 1850, life in China had become unbearable for many people. Between 1740 and 1850, the population of China grew from about 160 million to 430 million. Poor peasants struggled to raise enough food. At the same time, Europeans demanded to trade at Chinese ports. The British, finding China didn't want their industrial products, sold opium to the Chinese. In 1810, there were ten million opium addicts in China. These addicts spent their money on the drug. They grew thin, sickly, and pale. They didn't have the energy to work. Opium ruined many Chinese peoples' lives. Opium was expensive too. Money and goods poured out of China to Western countries in exchange for opium. The Qing government banned opium sales but, in 1840, the British, the United States, and some European powers sent warships to Chinese harbors. The Qing forces were defeated. The foreigners won concessions—the right to their own trading ports on the seacoast and the Yangzi River. Then, Westerners demanded money to pay for the costs of fighting the war. Peasants, already stretched to their limits, would have to pay for the concessions through higher taxes. They had had enough.

In 1850, Hong Xuanjiao's brother, Hong Xiuquan, had a vision about ridding the earth of demons. He had learned about Christianity and came to believe he was the second son of the Christian God. He believed he was meant to create a better world, a "Kingdom of Heaven" on earth. He called for Chinese people to fight the Qing. He declared men and women equal. He recruited women to his army. Hong Xuanjiao became one of his strongest supporters. Thousands of peasants, tired of starving while the wealthy lived pampered lives, joined the cause—the Taiping Rebellion.

The Taipings fought their way north from Guangxi Province. Two years later, they set up their capital at Nanjing. At their strongest, the Taiping rebels controlled most of southern China. By 1853, ten thousand women had joined the rebellion. They ate together and lived separately from the men. They were organized into groups with different duties. Some made bamboo traps to slow the enemy. Some carried bricks to build forts. Others wound hemp into ropes to trip enemy horses, or measured and distributed grain from the common storehouse that supported the revolutionaries.

Hong Xuanjiao led the women's army. Taiping women warriors were ferocious. She must have been proud when the women's battalions defeated government troops. She led a women's army in the Nuipai Mountains where Taiping troops ambushed and killed one thousand Qing soldiers. Hong Xuanjiao's husband was also a leader in the rebellion. When he was killed in battle at Changsha, Hong Xuanjiao knew what she had to do. She put aside her grief and anger, took command of the battle, and led Taiping forces to victory.

Hua Mulan

Most stories about Hua Mulan agree that she was born in China's central plains at the end of the Period of Disunion (220–589 CE). Hua Mulan's father was called to serve in the army, but he was too old and sick to be a fighter. Sometimes a boy could take his father's place, but Hua Mulan's little brother was too young to go. So Hua Mulan disguised herself as a man and took her father's place. She and her family could be punished if anyone found out she was a woman. She kept her secret and fought heroically. After years in the army, Hua Mulan had become a famous general. The emperor offered Hua Mulan a high position, but she asked for a good horse instead. Then she rode home to her village. Later, her fellow soldiers discovered the brave general, who dressed like a man, was really a woman.

Hong Xuanjiao must have felt satisfied at how far the revolution had come. She and her companions may have sat up late at night imagining a future where peasants could keep their crops and foreigners didn't bring opium and soldiers into China. They looked forward to a China ruled by Chinese instead of Manchu people. The hope for a utopia, a heaven on earth, justified the brutal fighting. Hong Xuanjiao would have had painful memories of dead and dying soldiers, of ruined towns, and trampled fields. But it must have seemed worth the price. Chinese people were taking control of their lives.

As the Taiping rebellion gathered strength, European nations feared the rebels would win. European powers, with their destructive weapons, joined with the Qing government to put down the rebels. The war turned, to favor the Qing. In 1864, Qing troops captured the Taiping capital at Nanjing. The rebellion had lasted fourteen years. Twenty million people had died. In the final days of the war, thousands of Taiping rebels were killed, including Hong Xuanjiao's brother, Hong Xiuquan. No one knows what happened to Hong Xuanjiao.

Cixi, the Empress Dowager

End of the Empire
1835–1908
Qing Dynasty 1644–1912

During the Qing dynasty, Manchu families were required to register their daughters with the local government authorities when they became teenagers. Some girls from this list would be chosen to be servants or concubines at the Imperial Palace. Cixi's Manchu family entered her name on the register, beginning a process that changed history.

Cixi's father was a Qing official. Although the Qing rulers adopted Chinese customs and governmental form, the Qing dynasty was not Chinese. The Manchu had conquered China, and many Chinese resented them. Qing rulers appointed Manchu officials and used banner men, loyal Manchu soldiers, to keep China under Manchu authority.

The Manchu emperors ruled China from Beijing's Imperial Palace. Their officials chose the most beautiful and promising girls from the best Manchu families to enter the palace life. These women would be more loyal to the government than Chinese women. Manchu servant girls, perhaps chosen for their strength and health, could work harder too. They did not have bound feet as many Chinese girls did, and so they could do more chores without pain. A few exceptional girls were chosen to be concubines to the emperor.

Cixi was beautiful. She was picked to become one of the emperor's concubines. Cixi left her family and traveled with an official escort to the center of Beijing. She approached the walls of the Imperial Palace, from the north. Women entered the city through this gate, which led to the women's and servant's quarters. From now on, Cixi's life would be enclosed by these walls. She knew she might never see her family again.

The lavish palaces and gardens of the Imperial Palace would have awed a girl from even the finest Manchu family. Few ordinary people had ever seen it. Yellow tile roofs glowed above red walls. Carved dragons, with their imperial five toes, perched on the roofs. Cixi could count nine rows of nails shining in each door. The number nine meant long life. When she reached her destination, the women's quarters, she probably wished she could see more. The emperor's city was truly grand.

Now new experiences filled her life. She joined a household of dozens of women from which the emperor could choose a companion. These women were trained in court manners, calligraphy, or painting. They had their own tutors. There were shimmering silk gowns, perfumes, and hair ornaments to wear. But there was more to her new life than being pampered and trained.

Older Women
Confucian philosophy honored age. A woman gained control over the household's younger women by growing older. A young woman serving her mother-in-law knew that one day she would have daughter-in-laws of her own. Her adult sons would honor her and seek her advice and approval. An older widow might be the true power in the family.

Cixi would have been immediately surrounded by the concerns of court life. Which minister had the most power? Would she find a friend she could trust? Which concubine or wife would bear the emperor a son and heir? Who was his favorite?

Cixi learned well. She became a favored concubine. When she was twenty-one, in 1856, she gave birth to the emperor's only son. She had been in the court long enough to know what power this might give her. In 1857 she was given the title Honored Consort.

Even though she lived entirely within the walls of the Imperial Palace, as Honored Consort she was allowed to read reports that came to the emperor. She knew that across the empire, the Chinese people were rebelling against the Manchu rulers. She must have heard about the tremendous battles to the south where the Taiping Rebellion raged. Did she believe the rumor that the Taiping rebels could create new soldiers just by cutting magic paper? Maybe she worried about the China her son would inherit. She would have learned that foreign countries were demanding more of China's territory.

In 1860, Cixi's life changed again. English and French soldiers marched on the capital and the court fled the Imperial Palace. In 1861, before they could return, Emperor Xianfeng died. Cixi's five-year-old son, Tongzhi, became the emperor of China. Someone had to rule for him. Cixi struggled for power with Xianfeng's official wife, the Empress Xi An, and three princes. Finally, Cixi, Empress Xi An, and Prince Gong, a powerful member of the court, ruled as joint regents, sharing responsibility for the government.

Now Cixi sat behind the screen while the child emperor received court visitors. She listened intently to the minister's plans for building armies to fight the rebels. She whispered instructions to the little boy as he sat on the throne. She agreed that more young men should take the examinations for government service. She approved the purchase of modern weapons from foreign countries, to use against peasants who were rebelling in the north and the south. She made alliances with princes and generals. But she did not change the way China was ruled. The empire would continue as it always had.

Cixi's son Tongzhi, died when he was nineteen. Cixi moved quickly, working with a powerful general, to have her three-year-old nephew, Guangxu, installed as emperor. As they had for Tongzhi, Cixi and Empress Xi An acted as his regents. Cixi became more powerful and Xi An more quiet. In 1880, Xi An died. Now, although she didn't hold the emperor's title, Cixi ruled China. She was called the Empress Dowager.

Dragon and Phoenix

The symbol of the Qing emperors was a five-clawed dragon. This dragon symbolized rain, good fortune, and the power of Heaven on Earth. Empresses were represented by the phoenix, a mythical bird, whose head, body, feet, and tail combined the parts of many birds and animals. The phoenix appeared only in times of peace. At the end of the 1800s, the Qing dynasty struggled to keep control over China. The dragon (Qing power) and the phoenix (peace) would soon disappear. Between the years of the Opium War of 1840 and the revolution that established the People's Republic of China in 1949, many wars followed, one after the other. Millions of Chinese women and men died in battle, starved, lost homes and fields, were executed, or became refugees. Some historians estimate that the population of China may have dropped by sixty million people during this time.

The empress dowager had easily controlled her son, Tongzhi. Her nephew, Guangxu, when he grew old enough to speak for himself, was different. Guangxu wanted to change China. During the more than two hundred years that the Qing dynasty ruled China, the world had changed. Europeans colonized the Americas, parts of Asia, and Africa. Revolutions in the United States, France, Mexico, and South America set the stage for new kinds of governments. Trains crossed continents and ships crossed oceans bringing people and ideas together. Political thinkers such as Voltaire, Rousseau, and Marx wrote about people governing themselves. Slaves, farmers, workers, and women began to demand better treatment and political power. Despite the Qing laws against leaving China, thousands of Chinese headed for Southeast Asia, California, Hawaii, Cuba, Canada, and other places hoping to improve their fortunes.

Emperor Guangxu came of age and took over the Qing government in this new world. Foreign powers were pushing at China's borders. In 1894, the Japanese attacked Korea and north China. Money meant for the Chinese navy had been spent to build a new summer palace for Cixi. The Chinese navy also discovered that some of its gun shells were filled with sand instead of gunpowder. The Chinese lost this war and then borrowed money from European nations to pay for it.

By 1898, Japan, Russia, Germany, France, Britain, and the United States were all demanding pieces of China. They built railroads, ports, and mines in areas of the country that they controlled. China was being divided up and given away. The Qing government didn't seem able to stop it. Educated Chinese demanded that China change. Emperor Guangxu supported reforms in education and government that could help China cope in the modern world. In 1898, he began a series of changes called the "hundred days of reform." Cixi did not want reform. She had Guangxu arrested and locked in his palace quarters.

In 1900, another uprising, the Boxer Rebellion, threatened the Qing dynasty. Peasants blamed foreigners for their troubles. They began attacking foreign missionaries and troops. Cixi was caught in the middle. She needed the support of the Chinese people to continue to rule, but peasants were always rebelling. There had been many peasant rebellions since she'd moved to the palace as a girl.

She needed the foreigners' support, too. She armed her troops with foreign weapons. The weapons and foreign-built railroads helped her keep China under Manchu control. She made a practical decision. Cixi encouraged the Boxer rebels to fight the foreigners. Then she sent her soldiers to protect the foreigners in their compounds. For a time, both sides believed she was helping them.

During the Boxer Rebellion, Western armies—German, English, French, and American—captured Beijing. Cixi and the court fled the Imperial Palace a second time. Still, Manchu rule continued. The Chinese signed a peace treaty with the foreigners and Cixi returned to the Imperial Palace. The imperial court arrived in Beijing by special train and then, in an impressive parade, Emperor Guangxu, Cixi, and and other officials were carried through the streets in sedan chairs while Chinese and Manchu soldiers knelt and commoners were told to stay inside.

Now Cixi ruled in front of the screen. She invited the ladies of the foreign delegations to visit her at court. Manchu princesses even accepted a return invitation, venturing out of the Imperial Palace to visit the home of the head of the delegation of the United States.

Cixi began her own reforms. She had to keep control somehow. Foreigners seeking empires, peasants hungry for food, and educated Chinese who demanded a "new China" were a threat to the dynasty. She allowed reforms in education, and encouraged study of modern sciences. The Qing sent delegations to other countries to study their constitutions. In 1908, Qing officials registered some educated men to vote in future elections. But the reforms Cixi allowed came too late. The Qing dynasty could not control China. Foreigners still dominated much of China. Chinese people wanted to get rid of the Manchu and rule their own country. Many upper-class Chinese had studied abroad and seen how other countries were run. Chinese people wanted change.

Emperor Guangxu died in 1908. The Empress Dowager died the next day. When she died, China was left with a new boy emperor and weak officials. In 1911, a revolution would end the Chinese empire. It would succeed, in part, because the Empress Dowager was gone.

Qiu Jin

Feminist
1879–1907
Qing Dynasty 1644–1912

Qiu Jin was born in 1879 in Zhejiang Province on the east coast of China. As a girl, she learned Chinese boxing, horsemanship, and fencing. She learned to read and write, and studied Chinese classics and literature. Then she was married to a wealthy merchant and moved to Beijing. Becoming a wife was probably difficult for an independent woman like Qiu Jin. Before, she had been active and educated. Now, she was expected to do as her husband said. In her new home, Beijing, she began to meet people who were concerned about what was happening in China.

After the Opium War and Taiping Rebellion, European traders and soldiers had moved deeper into China. Western missionaries took peasant lands for their churches and wanted special treatment from government officials. Japan had seized Manchuria and the island of Taiwan. The Chinese were worried that the empire would be broken up into colonies controlled by foreigners.

In 1900, a group of religious kickboxers, believing their sacred martial arts movements protected them from harm, started a rebellion (the Boxer Rebellion) against the foreigners. Boxer women formed fighting units—the most famous was called the Red Lanterns. They used swords and fans in their routines. During the war, Boxer women nursed the injured, spied on the enemy, burned foreign buildings, and fought alongside Boxer men. The Qing government joined the Boxers, for a time, hoping to rid itself of foreign abuse. Eight Western countries, including England, France, the United States, and Germany, fought to stop the Boxers. The foreigners won. They embarrassed and punished the Qing government.

Qiu Jin lived in the capital during the Boxer Rebellion. She saw how Chinese troops were defeated and humiliated by European forces. She saw foreigners attack and destroy sections of her Beijing. It made her angry.

In the years after the Boxer Rebellion, Qiu Jin began to believe, as did many young, upper-class Chinese, that there was only one way for China to survive. Chinese people needed education. They needed to get rid of the Qing emperors, and they needed to modernize. Qiu Jin believed China needed Western knowledge in order to protect itself from the foreigners. She also believed that women's rights were a key to changing China. "Without educating women we can't have a strong nation," she said. "Without women's rights our nation will remain weak." In 1904, she made a bold change. She sold her jewelry, ran away from her abusive husband, and traveled with a friend to Japan. She was free of her husband and his demands. She was going to a foreign country. It must have seemed like a great adventure. But Qiu Jin was serious about what she was doing. She was determined to study at the university in Japan.

> **Students and Revolution**
>
> In Chinese tradition, scholars had a responsibility to share their knowledge with the government. Dynasties needed the blessing of scholars to gain the right to rule. So it isn't surprising that students and reformers called for modern education and revolution at the same time.

Once she arrived in Japan, she joined a group of revolutionary Chinese students. Together they spent hours talking about how they would change things when they went back to China. The meetings were intense. They were also probably comforting for students living far from home. Through the group, Qiu Jin met Dr. Sun Yatsen, who was organizing a revolution against the Qing dynasty. He appointed her to be the revolutionary leader for her province, Zhejiang. Qiu Jin went to work while she was still in Japan. She began the revolutionary movement's first women's organization. Qiu Jin was easy to recognize. She gave passionate speeches, dressed in men's clothing, and carried a dagger.

In 1906, Qiu Jin returned to China to teach and organize for the revolution. It was dangerous to oppose the Qing government. People who spoke out could be beaten, arrested, or killed. But fear didn't stop her. Qui Jin started a magazine, *Chinese Women's Journal (Zhonggua Nubao)*. The magazine called for the education of women. Qiu Jin also wanted the revolutionaries to create a Chinese women's association that would help women claim their rights.

"The revolution must begin inside the family," Qiu Jin wrote. "This means equal rights for men and women." This idea was new, extreme, and dangerous. Even modern-thinking Chinese men would be angered by her demands for changes in the family.

Qiu Jin pushed on. In 1907 she was part of a group that built bombs and plotted an uprising against the government. The plot was discovered by the Qing government. Qiu Jin was captured and executed. But the movement for a new China, for which she had given her life, would not be stopped. In 1911, after several years of uprisings in South China, Dr. Sun Yatsen's forces brought down the Qing government.

Sun Yatsen

Sun Yatsen, born in 1866 in Guangdong, grew up hearing stories of the heroes of the Taiping Rebellion. When he was a teen, his family sent him to Hawaii to live with his brother and attend school. After Sun returned to China he became a Christian and studied medicine. Sun Yatsen had lived in the West and he believed the Qing dynasty was holding China back and allowing its people to be abused by landlords and foreigners. He wanted to change this. So in 1894 he returned to Hawaii and began a secret revolutionary society. This was the first of many revolutionary groups and governments he would lead. After participating in a failed uprising in Guangdong he fled to Japan. There he organized thousands of patriotic Chinese students, such as Qiu Jin. The idea was that they would lead a revolution when they returned home. Sun traveled to England, the United States, and Japan raising money and support for a revolution against the Qing dynasty.

Xiang Jingyu

Revolutionary Martyr
1895–1928

Xiang Jingyu was the daughter of a successful businessman from Xupu, Hunan. In 1902, when she was seven, cholera spread through her part of China. People in a nearby town believed the disease came from poisoned water. They accused two British missionaries and their housekeeper of poisoning a well. A mob attacked and killed the missionaries.

The British demanded that the Qing government punish the mob. Three hundred people were arrested and ten were executed. This punishment made many people in Hunan angry at both the foreigners and the Qing government. As a little girl, Xiang Jingyu might not have understood everything that happened, but she must have known how outraged and scared the adults around her were.

Then, Xiang Jingyu's brother went away to study in Japan. There, he backed Dr. Sun Yatsen who was organizing support for a revolution among Chinese students and businessmen living overseas. When her brother returned to China, he encouraged Jingyu to imagine a new China where life would be different.

Xiang Jingyu was able to go to school, too. Since the 1840s, missionaries from the United States and European countries had opened schools for girls as well as boys. Many modern Chinese families sent their daughters to these schools. Her teachers told the students they should learn so they could help educate others. She took their advice to heart. She must have believed her actions could help change the world.

In 1916, Xiang Jingyu, who was now twenty years old, opened a girls' school in her hometown, Xupu. She hoped her students would be part of China's new citizenry. Xiang Jingyu met other young Chinese who wanted change. She joined organizations that proposed a "new China." She spoke out against footbinding, which crippled many Chinese women.

Then, once again, actions by foreigners shocked China. European powers, negotiating the end of World War I in Europe, agreed to "give" China's Shandong Peninsula to Japan. The Europeans gave away this piece of China as a reward for Japan's support in the war. The Chinese felt betrayed. They organized to stop trade with Japan.

The Republic of China and the New Culture Movement

The empire was gone, but the new China, where life was modern and people had opportunities to make their lives more secure, was still a dream. China was a large and complex place. The new Republic of China was centered in southern China with Guangzhou as its capitol. It was directed by Sun Yatsen's political party, the Nationalists. But warlords controlled Beijing and much of central China, and foreign governments hoped to increase their power within China. There was fighting and confusion. After 1911, many people, especially students and intellectuals, argued for more changes. Through books, magazines and organizations, and discussion groups, they criticized traditional Confucian culture, saying that China would not make progress until people moved to new ways of thinking and organizing themselves. China's new society should be democratic, and based on science.

On May 4, 1919, three thousand Chinese students demonstrated in Tiananmen Square in Beijing. They burned the house of the Chinese ambassador to Japan, demanding that the Japanese leave the country. Newly installed telegraph lines carried the news to other cities. The demonstrations spread. Sixty thousand factory workers in Shanghai went on strike. Across the country, Chinese people began to demand changes. In Hunan, Xiang Jingyu joined the demonstrations. She helped organize rallies in Changsha. At the gatherings, she spoke out against the local warlord. Her father decided she was making too much trouble. She could bring disaster to the family. He believed the best way to control her was to get her married, so he arranged for her to marry an army commander. But Jingyu refused. No one realized it then, but the demonstrations that began May 4th would mark a turning point for China.

Like many young Chinese she believed it was necessary to challenge both European powers and Chinese traditions. Confucian ideas about the family and the role of women would have to change. Women should be allowed to marry whom they wished.

Women should be able to have jobs and own land as men did. Women should be able to speak out in public, and be heard in the new government. To an educated woman like Xiang Jingyu, an arranged marriage represented what was wrong with China.

Xiang Jingyu took a bold step. She moved out of her parents' house and into the home of a young political leader, Cai Heseng, and his sister Cai Chang. This house was a gathering spot for local activists (including China's future leader, Mao Zedong). They studied and debated. They talked about Russia, where the people had defeated the tsars and had built a new government and a new way of life. What could China learn from this?

Xiang Jingyu wanted to learn more. She and Cai Chang were able to join a work-study plan for young Chinese arranged by the French government. They left for France. The Chinese students worked ten-hour days in factories, ate cheap food, and lived in crowded rooms. They studied French and talked late into the night about what was happening in China. Although there was a new government run by Sun Yatsen's political party, the Peoples' Nationalists Party (also known as the Nationalists, Guomindang or Kuomintang, KMT), China was still held back by warlords and foreign powers. Which groups could be organized to overthrow them?

> **People's Nationalist Party**
>
> In 1921, Dr. Sun was made leader of the revolutionary government. He reorganized the Nationalist party to fight for a new society according to his "Three Peoples' Principles": national freedom, democratic government, and livelihood for the people. Russia sent advisors to help the Nationalists organize and train an army that could free the rest of China. The newly-formed Communist Party of China cooperated with the Nationalists.

They also compared the lives and rights of Chinese women with women in other countries. In modern, democratic countries, like the United States, women were winning the right to vote. Chinese women were still subjected to footbinding and forced marriages. Yes, they needed education. But did women need to demand more?

Life in France wasn't all work and discussions. Xiang Jingyu and Cai Heseng got married. He was a member of the new Communist Party of China. Xiang Jingyu joined too. In the still-tiny party, there was talk of big changes for women. The organization stated that

China couldn't change unless the situation of women changed. Many young Chinese women were attracted to the Communist Party. Here, they were listened to. There was work for them to do.

In 1922, Xiang Jingyu was back in Shanghai, China. She was the new director of the Chinese Communist party's Women's Bureau. Now she was responsible for planning and organizing the party's work with women. Xiang Jingyu knew that if Chinese women were educated, and allowed to work and make their own decisions, almost every family in China would have to change. Traditional men really hated the idea. Even the communist men she worked with didn't always support women having freedoms. And Xiang Jingyu had her own problems. She had a both a demanding new job and a new baby. She took her baby to Hunan to be cared for by her in-laws. Once there, she found her own family was ill. They expected her to stay and help them. She stayed in Hunan for several months before returning to work in Shanghai.

Other Chinese women activists in the 1920s were caught between their life in traditional China and their desire to have new roles in a new China. Some women committed suicide to avoid unhappy marriages while others were executed for revolutionary activities. Many women, still in their teens, were thrown in jail or killed for demanding change. Xiang Jingyu and other leaders had to find ways to help. They needed to make a plan of action.

Xiang Jingyu was strong, independent, and capable. She often had different ideas from other leaders, including her husband. Her marriage fell apart and she left him. Despite her success as

Communist Party of China
The Communist Party of China (Chinese Communist party, CPC) was formally established in Shanghai in 1921 by a small group of young Chinese inspired by the successes of the Russian Revolution. (Mao Zedong was one of them.) The ideas of Marx and Lenin seemed to offer the clearest way to a better future for the workers and peasants of China. Initially, CPC members primarily worked to educate and support factory workers who were struggling for higher wages, better working conditions, and basic rights. The CPC also joined with the Nationalist party to oppose warlords and foreign control of China. But China was an agricultural country. Most people were peasant farmers, not urban workers. After 1927, the CPC would change its strategy to concentrate on organizing rural people.

a leader in the Chinese Communist party, she was removed from her job and sent to Russia "for training." Xiang Jingyu returned to China in 1927, just as the government, led by the Nationalist party, turned against the Communists. Although the Nationalists had worked with the Communists in the past, now Nationalist soldiers rounded up hundreds of Chinese Communist party members—workers, students, peasant leaders, and other activists. They killed thousands of people in the streets and in their villages. In 1928, at age thirty-three, Xiang Jingyu was arrested and executed.

Women in the 1911 Revolution
During the 1911 revolution, women printed posters, nursed the sick, and joined the Red Cross. Some women formed fighting regiments in the army and navy. They fought in Nanjing, Shanghai, and Guangzhou.

Woman Students and Revolution
In the 1920s, high school and college girls were eager to be included in the new China they dreamed of. They formed women's associations to work for a new government and women's freedom. Members of women's associations marched in the streets, or put on plays in the countryside about women being able to choose their own marriage partners. They cut their hair to show their rebellion against traditional women's roles. They published newspapers about women's rights. In the end, they supported rebel armies, and pushed through laws against footbinding and selling servant girls.

Soong Qingling

Idealist for the People
1893–1981

Soong Qingling grew up in a wealthy home in Shanghai. Her father, Charlie Soong, was a businessman who had become a Christian. He made his fortune printing inexpensive Chinese-language bibles. Her mother was from a well-established Chinese Christian family. She knew English, played the piano, and cooked Western food. Soong Qingling's household was filled with activity. Qingling had an older sister, a younger sister, and little brothers. Her father's friends, business partners, and political associates were always coming and going.

When Soong Qingling was seven years old, she began her education at a respected, foreign-run, mission school in Shanghai. Dressed neatly in a western-style uniform, she joined her older sister and the other girls who lived and studied at the McTyeire School.

Soong Qingling was too young to understand that foreign Christian missionaries had enraged many Chinese with their demands and attitudes. For Soong Qingling, missionaries were part of everyday life. Her own family was Christian. As a boy, her father had worked as a sailor. He had been taken in by a missionary who educated him in the United States. Girls like Qingling went to mission schools.

But the Soong household was far from ordinary. While Qingling was learning to get along in school, her father was helping to organize a revolution against the Qing dynasty. He provided money and printed leaflets and posters for the revolutionaries. He was a close friend of Dr. Sun Yatsen, the man who would be called the "father of the Chinese revolution."

Life was dangerous for Charlie Soong and his family. If the Qing authorities learned about his activities he might be arrested and executed. In 1907, when Qingling was fourteen, Charlie Soong arranged for her and her younger sister, Meiling, to leave China to attend school in New Jersey. They would be safer there. Their older sister, Ailing, was already at school in the United States. Qingling was a serious girl with a love for her country. She was excited to go away to school, but sorry to leave when everyone around her seemed to be struggling to build a new, modern China.

Qingling studied in the United States for five years, first in New Jersey, then at Wesleyan College in Georgia. A good student, she went by her English name, Rosamunde. Although thousands of Chinese students were now going overseas for their educations, few were women. Qingling and Meiling were the only Chinese girls at their schools. Meiling made friends easily, but calm, studious Qingling spent her time thinking and writing.

Qingling's father wrote to her often, describing what was happening in China. She was extremely interested in the unfolding revolution. In 1911, the whole world learned that Chinese revolutionaries led by Dr. Sun Yatsen had overthrown the Qing government and declared China to be a republic. China was no longer an empire. In Georgia, Qingling celebrated.

The revolutionaries of 1911 didn't have the power to take control of the whole country. China was weak from decades of rebellion and foreign wars. In the countryside, local warlords, with their private armies, were often the real rulers. Foreign governments controlled large sections of Chinese territory. In the cities, factions within the new government struggled with each other for control. Fighting broke out between generals and politicians over who would rule.

Qingling graduated in 1913 and headed home. But she rejoined her family in Japan, not Shanghai. Her father's friend and revolutionary co-conspirator, Dr. Sun Yatsen, had briefly been in charge of the new Chinese republic's government. But Sun was replaced by an army general, Yuan Shikai. When Yuan began making many government decisions by himself, Sun Yatsen said Yuan was acting like an emperor. Dr. Sun called for the people to overthrow Yuan Shikai too. Yuan intended to arrest Sun Yatsen. Soong Qingling's father realized he and his family might be arrested, as well. Hastily, Sun Yatsen and the Soong family had fled China for the safety of Japan.

Qingling's older sister, Ailing, had been Dr. Sun's English-language secretary. While they were living in Japan, Ailing got married, so Qingling took over her old job. Soong Qingling worked side by side with Sun Yatsen as he tried to regain control of the revolution and get rid of Yuan Shikai. It was an intense time. Each day must have been both exciting and frustrating. They became very close and soon they began a romance. Qingling's father disapproved of their relationship. Sun Yatsen was almost fifty and Soong Qingling was only twenty. Besides, Sun had been married before.

Qingling's father took her and the family back to Shanghai. He arranged for her to marry another man and he locked her in her room. Secretly, Soong Qingling made plans to return to Japan to join Sun Yatsen. One night, in October 1915, she escaped by climbing down a ladder from her bedroom window, and she sailed to Japan. Soong Qingling and Sun Yatsen were married the day after she arrived. Her family was furious.

In Japan, Soong Qingling worked closely with her husband as he raised money and support for a new revolution that would create a government for Chinese people, not generals. It was unusual for a Chinese woman to take on a public role. It was very unusual for a wife of a political figure. Sun Yatsen and Soong Qingling worked with revolutionaries, idealistic students, and demanding generals. They met with foreigners who supported their goals. In 1916, Yuan Shikai died. Sun Yatsen and Soong Qingling returned to China.

Soong Qingling believed that women must be freed from the demands of traditional Chinese society in order for the revolution to succeed. She lived by that idea. Qingling was often in the public eye, poised, confident, and strong. She spoke out on important issues. She pushed to establish the Nationalist party's Women's Department, and became its head. She and Sun lived simply, paying little attention to decorating their rooms, or cooking elaborate meals. Their lives were often in danger. Many times, they escaped capture and death by a hair, crawling through alleys or traveling in disguise. In 1922, she suffered a miscarriage after a harrowing escape from a warlord's army.

Even at the worst of times, Soong Qingling firmly believed China could become a strong nation whose people had a say in their future. Sadly, Sun Yatsen would not live to see it. In 1925, he died of cancer. Soong Qingling and Sun had been inseparable for ten years. Qingling mourned. But not for long. She vowed to continue with the work to change China.

The fighting for China continued. Farmers were revolting against landlords who claimed up to seventy percent of their crops. Factory workers protested horrible working conditions.

> **Who Supported What?**
> Chinese people supported Nationalists and Communists for different reasons. Nationalists were more traditional. Generally, merchants, landowners, and upper-class city people supported the Nationalist party. Communists wanted to change the way society was arranged. Poor people, workers, peasants, and intellectuals were more likely to support the communists.

The Chinese Communist party now had many members. In 1926, the Nationalist party, supported by the Communists, decided it was time to try to take control of more of China. It began a military expedition toward the north, led by General Chiang Kai-shek (also known as Jiesi or Jiang Zhongzhen). The going, against unpopular warlords, was fairly easy, and soon the government established a capital at Wuhan, a big city on the Yangzi River. It must have seemed that the new government would win all of China. Soong Qingling was now a leader in the Nationalist party and the government, and she joined other officials there. She concentrated on issues that affected women. She started a school to train women political workers. She worked to rescue and protect "child brides" and child servants. She made speeches. Because she was Sun's widow, she received a lot of attention. Newspapers wrote about her. Her opinion was sought. She was often portrayed as if she was a fierce soldier, gun in hand, leading a charge. But Soong Qingling's power came from her gentle, composed manner. And it came from her unwavering belief in a better future.

The cooperation between the Nationalists and the Chinese Communists began to break down. Chiang Kai-shek was now the leader of the Nationalists. His group set up a separate headquarters at Nanjing, another major city on the Yangzi. More than once, Soong Qingling publicly criticized the Nationalists. In 1927, Nationalist troops attacked striking workers in Shanghai, killing hundreds of people in the streets. Then they moved to squash the

Communists. Chinese Communist party members and supporters were rounded up and massacred. (Soon, the Nationalists would do the same in Guangzhou.) Activists who survived fled to rural areas. Traditionalists and businessmen backed the Nationalists. Soong Qingling would not. She said their government was not working for the people. As the killings continued, she fled to Russia.

Her family was in the middle of the power struggle. That same year, 1927, Qingling's younger sister Meiling married Chiang Kai-shek. Her brother was a high official for the Nationalist party. General Chiang wanted Qingling's support for the Nationalist government. The Chinese Communist party wanted her blessing too. People admired Soong Qingling—and she was Dr. Sun Yatsen's widow. Her backing would be an important tool for any group trying to win China. Soong Qingling didn't believe either side represented her husband's ideals. Angering her family and old friends, she called for a social revolution that would allow the Chinese people to govern and work for themselves.

Soong Qingling returned from Russia in 1931 to find things worse than when she had left China. Many people were under arrest for opposing the Nationalist government. Soong Qingling responded by founding the China League for Civil Rights, to support political prisoners and defend civil rights. And there were other troubles. The Japanese government sent troops into northern China. The Nationalists didn't put up much resistance, and Japan gained control of China's northeast. Patriotic Chinese including Soong Qingling reacted, calling for the government and people to "resist Japan and save the nation."

In 1936, Nationalist military generals captured their own leader, Chiang Kai-shek, and forced him to agree to join with the Communists to fight Japan. But forming a United Front against Japan didn't stop the Nationalists from also fighting the Communists.

In 1937, Japan launched a full-scale invasion of China. The occupation was brutal. Japan's soldiers killed hundreds of thousands of ordinary Chinese. The Nationalist government fled west to Chongqing. Most of China came under Japanese control. The Communists fought back from their bases among the farmers of China's northwest. When Japan's troops captured Shanghai, Soong

Qingling escaped to England's colony of Hong Kong. There, she organized a new group, the China Defense League. It raised money and sent medical supplies and aid to anti-Japanese fighters in China. She spoke out for uniting people, governments, and countries to defeat Japan as a step toward world peace.

World War II
The fighting spread. In 1941, Japan attacked the U.S. naval bases in Hawaii and the Philippines, captured the Philippines, and the then-British colonies of Hong Kong, Burma (Myannmar), Singapore, and Maylaya (Malaysia). The United States and the European countries already fighting Germany in Europe were now drawn into the war against Japan. The Chinese people would no longer be fighting the powerful Japanese military alone.

As Japanese troops moved in to capture Hong Kong, Soong Qingling evacuated to Chongqing, where, she rebuilt the China Defense League. Soong Qingling worked tirelessly to raise money and organize support for the fight against Japan. She worked with everyone—military advisors and government representatives from the United States and Britain, patriotic Chinese, and Chinese Communist party leaders. She was, possibly, the best-known person in Chongqing. Qingling lived simply, on income from her pension as Sun Yatsen's widow. She couldn't afford a clock. The Nationalist authorities were waiting out the war, counting on the United States and its allies to defeat Japan. They didn't like her very much. But they needed her.

In 1945, Japan surrendered after the United States dropped atomic bombs on Hiroshima and Nagasaki. Now, who would rule China? The civil war, between the Nationalists and Communists intensified. By now, most ordinary Chinese, especially the peasant farmers, felt the Communists offered a better future than the Nationalists. The Communists had put up the best fight against the Japanese. They would end foreign control of China's resources. They already controlled parts of north China. In those areas, land was being redistributed to the farmers who actually worked it. Women got their own share. Poor farmers were encouraged, for the first time, to stand up for their rights. Schools were being organized for children. The Red (Chinese Communist) Army was made up of volunteers, not conscripts like the Nationalist army.

Red Army soldiers were taught to read and write. They knew what they were fighting for. The civil war lasted four years. In the end, despite better weapons and international support, the Nationalists were defeated. Chiang Kai-shek and his supporters (including Soong Qingling's family) fled to the island of Taiwan.

Soong Qingling would not go, even though she was offered a high government position with the Nationalists. On October 1, 1949, she stood with Mao Zedong, Zhou Enlai, Zhu De, and the others who had led the revolution, as the new Peoples' Republic of China was declared.

Soong Qingling was appointed to be a vice chairman of the central government. She was one of only three leaders who were not Chinese Communist party members. Her enormous prestige and her personality continued to give her authority, and she traveled the world representing China. In 1951, the Russian government awarded her a prize in honor of her work for world peace. With the money, she opened the first hospital for women in Shanghai. She also founded the China Welfare Institute. It provided day care, health services, and cultural programs for children. It also published a magazine in many languages introducing the new China to people of other countries.

Soong Qingling never remarried, but she adopted two girls. Until the end of her life, at age eighty-eight, she continued to work for the ideals she and Sun had set out to achieve so many years before. She wrote articles and met with all kinds of people. She was known for giving encouragement and support. Just before she died she was made an honorary member of the Communist Party of China. Today her Beijing home is a museum, visited daily by hundreds of ordinary people for whom she remains an inspiration.

Kang Keqing

*Revolutionary Soldier
1911–1992*

Kang Keqing was born on a fishing boat in 1911. Her parents were so poor that they gave her to a childless local farm couple. Like other girls in her village, Kang Keqing was put to work at an early age. By the time she was five, she was taking care of the family water buffalo.

In 1926, a Chinese Communist party organizer visited her village in Jiangxi Province. The river had flooded and crops had failed. The communists said peasants should unite to oppose the landlords and the taxes that kept the farmers in poverty. This made sense to Kang Keqing's father. He joined the communist cause, and became chairman of the village's Peasant Union. Kang Keqing longed for a way out of poverty too. She became leader of the Communist Youth organization in her village when she was fifteen.

Then, in 1927, the Nationalists began hunting for and killing communist leaders. Keqing and other village communist activists fled to the mountains. Kang Keqing survived, but a more ordinary problem faced her when she returned to her village. Her father had arranged a marriage for her.

But Kang Keqing had other plans. She was fascinated by the legends of Hua Mulan and had always wanted to be a soldier. In 1928, she joined the Red (Communist) Army. Most of the soldiers were men, but a few other women had joined. It was an all-volunteer army made up of young peasants with little training. It had no money for weapons. Soldiers fought with guns captured from the Nationalist troops they defeated. Very few of the soldiers could read or write, but they saw a better future with the communists. To her disappointment, Kang Keqing didn't get to fight. She was put to work organizing villagers and telling people about the Chinese Communist party's plans and views. She was a good organizer, and fearless.

That same year, Kang Keqing met the man she would marry. Zhu De was one of the most important Red Army commanders. He was also well educated and much older than she was—and he was her commander. So Kang Keqing was surprised when, in 1929, he asked her, an illiterate peasant girl, to marry him. Although she was concerned about their differences, Kang Keqing agreed. (It turned out to be a good match.)

She continued to work for the army. She organized a group of 180 peasant women into a fighting unit. However, they never fought a battle. Kang Keqing attended the Red Army Military Academy, but wasn't given a fighting assignment when she completed the course. Finally, her chance to fight came. She was traveling with a group of three hundred soldiers when they were attacked. She led the group in battle and earned the name, "The Girl Commander."

Kang Keqing was one of the few women selected to travel with the Red Army when it set out on the "Long March." In 1934, Nationalist troops were closing in on rural areas controlled by the communists. If the area was surrounded, everyone would be captured or killed. Red Army commanders decided to abandon their base in Jiangxi province and to try to outrun the Nationalist troops.

They left Jiangxi during the night. More than eighty-five thousand soldiers slipped away, deeper into the mountains. Thirty of them were women, all experienced organizers and activists.

The Nationalist army pursued the Red Army. At one point, they cut off the Red Army at a river crossing. Only about thirty thousand Red soldiers survived and managed to cross the river.

> **Women in the Revolution**
> Thousands of women participated directly in the fighting against the Japanese and the Nationalists. Some joined guerilla units guarding their villages behind enemy lines. Many joined the main Red Armies, working, like Kang Keqing, as organizers. One army branch, the Fourth Front, included an entire fighting battalion of woman soldiers. Women spun, wove, and sewed uniforms for the Red Army. They tended to the sick, often risking their lives to take injured soldiers to homes of people who supported the communists. Women discussed their new roles and supported each other in women's organizations. In areas controlled by the Red Army, they joined, and often led, the struggles to overthrow rich landlords and redistribute land to farmers.

The survivors, including Kang Keqing, kept walking. Crossing rugged southwest China, they climbed ten-thousand-foot mountains, slogged through swamps, and forded rivers. They walked, carrying all their gear, twenty miles a day or more. The soldiers fought battles, sometimes daily. Kang Keqing and the other soldiers went hungry for days at a time. Often the local villagers had no extra food to sell the soldiers. Sometimes fearful villagers hid from the army. It would take more than two years for the Long Marchers to reach a safe destination in North China.

Like Kang Keqing, many of the women on the Long March were married to military leaders. During the two years of the march, a few became pregnant and had babies. But the Long March was no place for a baby. A woman with a baby would have to drop out of the march. Hopefully she could find her way to safety. Some did drop out. Other women chose to leave their babies for local farmers to find and care for. There were no good choices. Even He Zizhen, the wife of Mao Zedong, left her new-born with farmers. The baby was never recovered.

A People's Army
Thirty thousand people could do a lot of damage to the fields and villages they passed through. The villagers were poor, too. The Red Army was ordered to treat the villagers well. If soldiers took food from villagers, they paid for it. Soldiers were taught a song, "The three points of attention and eight rules of discipline." They were to respect villagers, return what they borrowed, pay for what they took, and replace what they damaged. This was the first Chinese army in villagers' memory that didn't plunder villages. The farmers took note.

During the two years of the Long March, the Red Army dodged the Nationalist Army time and again. Finally, after walking eight thousand miles (thirteen thousand kilometers) the thirty thousand survivors arrived at Yan'an in the north. Communists had controlled this area for many years. Most villagers in the area supported them. It must have been a relief to finally stop walking. The soldiers settled into their new base. Kang Keqing and Zhu De moved into a traditional cave house, near other leaders. She had been illiterate until the revolution had come to her little village. Now she enrolled in the Chinese Communist party's university, to learn how to run a revolution, and, hopefully, a country. For relaxation, she played basketball. She was good, much better than her husband, and was always chosen before him for teams. But Kang Keqing still wanted her chance to fight.

There would be plenty of fighting to come. Two other big Communist armies, the First and Fourth Front Red Armies arrived in Yan'an in 1936. They had been on their own versions of the Long March. (The Fourth Front Army included a battalion of women fighters.) As Japan invaded and gained control of more and more of China, thousands of Chinese traveled from Japanese-controlled areas to Yan'an to join the fight. Kang Keqing was again put in charge of organizing villagers to find ways to resist the Japanese and help the Red Army.

She also found herself in an unfamiliar role. Patriotic Chinese such as Soong Qingling and advisors from the United States had pressured the Nationalists to cooperate with the Communists. Kang Keqing considered herself a soldier and ordinary person. She had always worn her army uniform, complete with pistol. Now she attended formal receptions and dinners with Nationalist officials. When these officials called her "Mrs. Zhu," she didn't know whom they meant.

Not long after the Japanese surrendered in 1945, the civil war between Nationalists and Communists resumed. The Nationalist soldiers were well armed. But the Nationalist government was not popular with the people who had lived under Japanese occupation. The Red Army was much smaller, and lacked modern weapons. But it was supported by most of China's rural people, and it was more skillful. In 1948, the Red Army took Beijing. The soldiers rode in American tanks captured from the Nationalists. Kang Keqing and other Communist leaders prepared for victory. On October 1, 1949, with the world watching, Mao Zedong declared "The Chinese people have stood up."

Kang Keqing was now a high official of the national government. She still saw herself as a military professional, who only wanted to be a commander. Instead, she was asked to work on child welfare with the newly-formed All China Women's Federation. She was to make plans that would improve health conditions for children, and develop childcare so women could hold jobs. Kang Keqing had never been interested in "the woman problem." She had always made her own way in a largely male world. But old traditions and habits were hard to end, and the new China expected competent women leaders to work with women on women's problems, not to lead armies. So Kang Keqing put aside her personal feelings. She had been working for this revolution since she was sixteen. She would do whatever was required of her.

The new Chinese government was already actively changing society. Landlords lost land and power over lives of ordinary people. Their land was redistributed to landless peasant families. Foreigners no longer controlled China's mines, factories, and railroads. Formerly illiterate poor peasant girls such as Kang Keqing herself could become national leaders.

But the government faced enormous challenges. Most of China's people were farmers and few people could read or write. Poverty, infectious diseases, and the lack of clean drinking water and health care caused millions of deaths. Floods and droughts caused more. China did not have the railroads, highways, electricity, or factories to supply what the country needed. Richer countries would not help. There were no successful models for the Chinese government to follow. In the years to come, China's leadership would make great progress but also make serious mistakes while trying to develop China and solve problems quickly. The outcome of bad policy decisions was, more than once, disastrous to millions of Chinese.

Cultural Revolution
The Cultural Revolution (1966–1976) grew out of a power struggle between Mao Zedong and other top leaders over the best ways for China to develop. Normal life was interrupted throughout China while people debated and fought, sometimes violently, over the proper road for China to follow to continue the revolution. Intellectuals, professional people and factory managers were publicly criticized for "old ideas," pulled from their jobs, and sent to the countryside to work and learn the hard life of farmers. Schools and universities were closed for several years. Passionate students, eager to clear the country of traditional thought, attacked teachers, took over schools, and destroyed antiques, books, and art works. Many people in leadership positions, including Long Marchers and others who had fought for the revolution, were publicly criticized, removed from jobs, and sometimes imprisoned.

Kang Keqing and her husband, Zhu De, were among the thousands of people targeted during the Cultural Revolution that began in 1966. She lost her job and the Women's Federation was closed down. She was humiliated in public. She must have felt bitter at being labeled an enemy after all she had done for her country. She and Zhu De spent the next few years at home, living quietly. But, again, she survived. Kang Keqing didn't give up on China.

In July 1976, Zhu De died, at age ninety. Several months later, Mao Zedong, China's top leader, died and new leadership took over. The Cultural Revolution officially ended. In 1978, Kang Keqing returned to her work. She was made chairperson of the Women's Federation. Now, at age sixty-seven, she had no hesitation about doing "women's work."

Before long, she realized how much work remained to be done. The illiteracy rate for women was still high. The Marriage Law was too often being ignored. And its guarantees didn't end discrimination. Old attitudes remained. Too many reports told of old ways—child brides, arranged marriages, and worse—continuing. Kang Keqing pushed for changes in the marriage law that would address the current situation. In 1980 she represented China at the United Nations Third Conference on the Rights of Women. She worked for policies that would outlaw discrimination against women. She spoke of women's self respect and dignity, and of the need for women to work in their own self-interest. She encouraged the Women's Federation to develop their own ideas on working with women, and on what was important. Finally, in 1984, in declining health, Kang Keqing retired. She died in 1992, at the age of eighty, a respected leader of her country who had never faltered in her belief that poor, illiterate, peasant girls, such as she had been, had a right to make their place in the world.

Marriage Law

One of the first laws passed by the new government was the Marriage Law. This law established equal rights for women. They could own property. They could choose their own husband. Women had a right to divorce. They had equal say in family matters. Under the new government, girls were encouraged to go to school. Women were encouraged to take jobs, both to earn their own money and to fully join society. But passing laws was one thing. Changing society was another, and it was much harder. Mao Zedong, who had led the revolution to power, said men had to struggle against old political, family, and religious rules, but women had to also struggle against men who controlled their lives.

Leaders

Mao Zedong helped found the Communist Party of China in 1921, became its major leader during the Long March, and held that position until his death in 1976. In the years after 1949, China's highest leaders were mainly the men who had led the Chinese Communist party from its beginnings to its victory. These included Mao Zedong, Zhu De, Zhou Enlai, who became China's Premier after 1949, and Deng Xiaoping, who would become China's main leader after the deaths of Mao and Zhou in the 1970s. Several other women besides Kang Keqing, also former Long Marchers, held posts at the next highest level. One, Cai Chang, the friend of Xiang Jingyu, headed the Women's Federation. Another, Deng Yingchao, was a former May Fourth student activist from Beijing who had married Zhou Enlai. Intelligent, hardworking and dedicated, she held many important government positions. Cai Chang and Deng Yingchao were also pushed out of their jobs during the Cultural Revolution. After the Cultural Revolution ended, Deng Yingchao was appointed to China's top leadership, and became the highest-ranking woman leader. When Mao Zedong launched the Cultural Revolution in 1966, his fourth wife, Jiang Qing gained political power and influence. She was asociated with some of the most extreme people and ideas of that period. The Cultural Revolution ended after Mao's death, and Jiang Qing and her allies were arrested. She was sentenced to a long prison term. In 1991, the Chinese government announced she had committed suicide.

Moving On

Since the 1980s, China's government has focused on policies intended to help China become strong, modern, and wealthy. Now, life in China, particularly in the cities, has become much as it is in more developed countries. Young girls grow up expecting to go to school, to earn enough money of their own to live comfortably, to voice their opinions, and choose their friends and husbands. Chinese women now study at the world's major universities, own and run high-tech businesses, compete successfully in the Olympics, and become international film stars. Chinese women hold every type of job. And China's government remains committed to achieving equality for women. In 1949 over ninety-five percent of women under age thirty-five were illiterate. Now, the rate is less than five percent. More than one half of women aged eighteen to sixty-five have at least a basic nine-year education. And the idea of equality between men and women is becoming accepted. According to national surveys, about two-thirds of China's women felt they had an equal say in all their family's big decisions, and almost all said they made their own personal decisions. More than eighty percent said they had faith in their own abilities. And eighty-eight percent agreed that men should share the housework!

But creating a more prosperous China causes new problems. Tradition can be hard to overcome, especially in the countryside, where many families still prize boys more than girls. Poverty still defines daily life in some areas of rural China. Today, more than ever, achieving success requires higher education. But many country girls do not, or cannot, continue on to high school. China's All-China Women's Federation activists still work to eliminate illiteracy among women. They help girls in China's poorest areas stay in school, and school dropouts return to school.

Some problems faced by Chinese women are familiar to people of more developed countries. In general, men earn more money than women. As industries modernize, older workers, especially women with little education and few job skills, face unemployment and are left behind. Thousands of young women leave their villages to find work in factories in south China. They work long hours, often without the protections of government or trade union rules, to make products for the rest of the world. While the money is good, compared to the countryside, living conditions are hard, and opportunities for training and advancement are few. The percentage of women government officials, although increasing, is still low. And well-educated, well-paid women wonder if a "glass ceiling" might block many of them from achieving full equality with men in the world of business and professions.

Newspaper articles discuss the growing gap between ordinary people and those who have become well-off. People fear that the good aspects of China's traditions can be lost in a rush to be like developed countries. They worry that some bad aspects of China's traditions might creep back in new disguises, and that young women, especially, might forget the lessons and sacrifices of the past.

But the future is exciting. Like women around the world, Chinese women will face new challenges and have new opportunities created by rapidly changing technologies, an increasingly smaller world, and changes that are inevitable as women empower themselves. Undoubtedly the women of today's China will go places and experience things they have yet to imagine.

A Folk Legend: Li Chi and the Monster

Long ago in China, a huge monster terrified the local people. One after another, he killed the area's strongest men. People offered him sheep and cows to eat, but they didn't satisfy the monster. Then he said, "If you want to save yourselves, send me young girls and I will eat them."

So each year, in the eighth month, the terrified people sent a girl, a daughter of a slave or criminal, to be sacrificed to the monster. He would then leave the villagers alone for another year. But as the eighth month neared, no girl felt safe. In the tenth year, Li Chi asked her parents if she might volunteer to meet the monster. Her parents loved her and refused, but Li Chi, feeling her life could never be worth more than if she saved her family a year of horror, secretly crept into town and volunteered to meet the monster.

"Give me a sword and a hunting dog, and I will go," she said. Sadly, the town officials agreed. Li Chi went to the monster's cave. She tempted him with sweet rice cakes, and when he crawled out to nibble them the hunting dog bit his neck and held fast. Li Chi jumped up behind him and cut him three, four, and five times with her sword. The monster shrieked, reared up, and then died.

Solemnly, Li Chi entered the monster's cave, bringing out the bones of the nine girls who had died before her. "How sad. Because you were afraid, you could not save yourselves." After that, no monster bothered the people. Li Chi gained riches and fame and her story is told to this day.

The Chinese Language and Pronunciation

This book uses the pinyin romanization system to write Chinese characters. This is the official system for standard Chinese used in the People's Republic of China, and generally used by U.S. newspapers and magazines. Books on Chinese history often use other, older systems of romanization. For example, instead of the pinyin spellings Zhou and Qing dynasties, Daoism and Beijing, you may see Chou, Ching, Taoism, and Peking.

Some letters are pronounced differently than English. Here is how to pronounce names in this book:

"a" as "a" in *father:* Shang, Shanghai, Tang, Han, Guomindang (Guo min dang)

"e" somewhat like *uh:* Wencheng (Wuhn chuhng)

"i" as in *he:* Jiangxi (Jee-ang shee)

(Double vowels are said together…try to make one sound).

"u" as "oo" in *food:* Fu Hao (Foo Hao)

"c" as "ts" as in *bats:* Cixi (Tsee-shee)

"zh" as "j" as in *jelly:* Zhou dynasty (Joe dynasty), Zhou Enlai (Joe un lie)

"q" as "ch" in *chew:* Soong Qingling (Soong Ching ling), Li Qingzhao (Lee Ching jao), Qiu Jin (Chway jin), Kang Keqing (Kang Ke ching)

"x" as "sh" in *sheet:* Zheng Zhenxiang (Juhng Juhn shi-ang), Xiang Jingyu (Shi-ang Jing yoo)

"z" as *ds:* Mao Zedong (Mao Dsuh dong), Wu Zetian (Woo Dse tian)

"Huang" is somewhat like *Wang:* Huang Daopo (Wang Dao po)

Chinese is a tonal language, and each character is pronounced with a specific tone (there are four). Characters with the same pinyin romanization may mean different things. Many internet sites provide an audio introduction to pinyin pronunciation and the tones of spoken Chinese.

Bibliography

China's History

Bray, Francesca. *Technology and Power: Fabrics of Power in Late Imperial China*. Berkeley: University of California Press, 1997.

Cass, Victoria Baldwin. *Dangerous Women: Warriors, Grannies, and Geishas of the Ming*. Lanaham, Md: Rowman & Littlefield, 1999.

Chang, Kwang-Chih. *Art, Myth and Ritual*. Cambridge, Mass: Harvard University Press, 1983.

Chang, Leslie T. *Factory Girls: From Village to City in a Changing China*. New York: Spiegal and Grau, 2008.

Chang, Y.N. *Giant Shadows, Small Footsteps*. Catskill, NY: Press Tige Publishing, 1998.

Ebrey, Patricia Buckley. *The Inner Quarters, Marriages and Lives of Chinese Women in the Sung Period*. Berkeley: University of California Press, 1993.

Epstein, Israel. *Woman in World History: Life and Times of Soong Qing Ling (Mme. Sun Yatsen)*. Beijing: New World Press, 1993.

Evans, Karin. *The Lost Daughters of China*. New York: Tarcher/Penguin, 2008.

Fairbank, John King. *China, A New History*. Cambridge, Mass: Harvard University Press, 1992.

Gernet, Jacque. *Daily Life in China on the Eve of the Mongol Invasion, 1250-1276*. Stanford, Calif: Stanford University Press, 1962.

Milwertz, Cecilia. *Beijing Women Organizing for Change: A New Wave of the Chinese Women's Movement*. Copenhagen: NIAS Press, 2002.

Tao Jie, Zheng Bijun and Mow, Shirley L., eds. *Holding Up Half the Sky: Chinese Women Past, Present and Future*. New York: The Feminist Press, 2004.

Women of China Series. *Departed but Not Forgotten*. Beijing: Women of China, 1984.

Xiao Hong Lee Lily and Wiles, Sue. *Women of the Long March*. St. Leonards, Australia: Allen & Unwin, 1999.

Zhong, Xueping, Zheng, Wang and Di, Bai, eds. *Some of Us: Chinese Women Growing Up in the Mao Era*. New Brunswick, NJ: Rutgers University Press, 2001.

Folklore, Fiction, and Memoirs

Chen, Chen. *Come Watch the Sun Go Home: A Memoir of Upheaval and Revolution in China.* New York: Marlowe, 1998.

Lin, Grace. *Where the Mountain Meets the Moon.* New York: Little Brown, 2009.

Jones, Teresa Chin. *Tales of the Monkey King.* Berkeley: Pacific View Press, 2008.

Roberts, Moss, ed. *Chinese Fairy Tales and Fantasies.* New York: Pantheon, 1979.

Wong, Jan. *Red China Blues: My Long March from Mao to Now.* New York: Doubleday, 1998.

A complete bibliography is available at *www.pacificviewpress.com*.

Index

Acupuncture 22
Ancestor, ancestors 7–11, 21, 37, 38, 40, 51
Anyang 7
Ban Zhao 17–19, 39
Baogu 21–23
Behind the screen 32–33, 65
Beijing 8, 55–57, 63, 67–70, 74, 85, 90, 93, 98
Bodhisattva 29
Biographies of Famous Women 39
Book of Han (Hanshu) 18
Boxer Rebellion 66–70
Brides 38–40, 44, 82, 92
Buddha, Buddhist 27–29, 31, 33, 57
Cai Chang 75, 93
Cai Heseng 75
Calligraphy, calligrapher 19, 33, 64
Chang'an 25, 27, 31, 44, 45
Changsha 60, 74
Chinggis Khan (Genghis Khan) 45
Chongqing 83–84
Christian, Christianity 45, 60, 71, 79
Cixi 63–67, 98
Colony, colonies, colonized 66, 69, 83, 84
Communist, Communist Party, Chinese Communist Party, CPC 75–77, 82–85, 87–90, 93
Concubine 31–35, 39, 56, 63, 64
Confucian (ideals, philosophy, culture) 17, 18, 23, 32, 33, 44, 49, 50, 57, 64, 74
Confucius 11, 15, 17, 18, 22, 51
Cotton 38, 45–46
Court (imperial) 18, 19, 25, 27, 31–35, 41, 46, 50, 56, 64, 65, 67
Courtesan 33
Cultural Revolution 91–93
Dancer, dancers 9, 33, 50
Dao, Daoism, Daoist 21–23, 50, 98
Daodejing (Tao Te Ching) 22

Deng Yingchao 93
Dian Wan 55
Double Seven Festival (Qi Xi) 47
Dowry 38–40, 51
Dragons 64, 65
Drought 56, 91
Du Fu 33
Earthquake, earthquakes 9, 34, 50
Education, educate 11, 14, 15, 17–19, 31, 33, 37, 66, 67, 69–71, 73, 75, 76, 80, 88, 94, 95
Embroider, embroidery 38, 47, 49, 51, 53
Emperor of Heaven 47
Empress Dowager 63, 65–67
Entertain, entertainer 9, 25, 31, 38, 49, 55, 56
Famine 9, 40, 56
Farm, farmers, farming 8, 13–15, 26, 27, 34, 38, 41, 43, 45, 46, 49, 66, 76, 82–84, 87–89, 91
Floods 9–11, 34, 87
Footbinding, bound feet 49, 50, 59, 63, 73, 75, 77
Foreign, foreigners 25, 26, 31, 37, 59, 61, 65–67, 69–71, 73–76, 79–81, 84, 91
Fu Hao 7–11, 98
Genghis Khan (Chinggis Khan) 45
Gongsun Daniang 33
Grain 8, 9, 21, 26, 38, 43, 60
Great Wall 56, 57
Guangdong 21, 23, 51, 59, 71
Guangxu 65–67
Guanyin 29
Guomindang (Kuomintang) 75, 98
Hainan Island 44–46
Hakka 59
Han, Han Dynasty 17–19, 26, 27, 34, 35, 39, 44, 57, 98
Hanshu (Book of Han) 18
Hawaii 66, 71, 84

Historian, historians 7, 17, 19, 34, 35, 65
Holeus 45
Hong Kong 83–84
Hong Xiuquan 60
Hong Xuanjiao 59–60
Hua Mulan 60, 87
Huang Daopo 43–47, 98
Imperial Palace 50, 56, 63–67
Intellectuals 74, 82, 91
Japan 66, 69–71, 73, 74, 80, 81, 83–84, 88, 90
Jiang Qing 93
Jiangxi 59, 87, 88, 98
Jin (Mongols) 40–41
Jin dynasty 21
Kang Keqing 87–93
Korea 25, 66
Kublai Khan 45
Landlord, landlords 71, 82, 87, 88, 91
Laozi 22
Lessons for Women (Nujie) 18–19, 39
Li people 44–46
Li Qingzhao 37–41, 98
Long March 88–91, 93
Luofu 35
Kuomintang (Guomindang) 75, 98
Madam Wei Shuo 19
Manchu, Manchus 56–57, 61, 63–64, 67, 69
Manchuria 57, 69
Mandate of Heaven 34, 50
Mao Zedong 75, 76, 85, 89–93, 98
Markets 15, 38, 49
Marriage 11, 13, 18, 25, 26, 28, 39–40, 50–51, 53, 75–77, 87, 92
Martial arts 22, 23, 69
May 4th, May Fourth Movement 74, 93
Medicine 10, 21–23, 27, 71
Mencius 14, 15, 17
Mengmu 13–15, 51
Merchants 49, 52, 69, 82
Ming dynasty 27, 49–53, 55–57
Missionary, missionaries 66, 69, 73, 79
Mongols, Mongolian 26, 40, 41, 43–45, 49, 50, 57

Nationalists, Nationalist Party 74–77, 81–85, 86–88, 90
Needlework 38, 47, 53
New China 8, 67, 71, 73, 74, 76–78, 90
Nie Yinnang 23
Nobles, noblemen 9, 11, 13, 14, 19
Nomads, nomadic 25–26, 45
Nu Wa 5
Nujie (Lessons for Women) 18–19, 39
Nushu (Women's Writing) 53
Opium 59, 61
Opium War 65, 69
Oracle inscriptions, oracle bones 7, 10
Pan Gu 5
Patriarchy 11
Peasants 45, 56, 59–61, 65–67, 76, 82, 87
People's Republic of China 8, 65, 98
Poet, poetry 17, 19, 33, 37, 39, 40, 49
Poverty, the poor 13, 15, 22, 38, 39, 43, 44, 46, 49, 51, 55, 59, 82, 84, 87, 89, 91, 92, 94
Prince Gong 65
Princess Wencheng 25–28, 31
Qi Xi (Double Seven) Festival 47
Qing dynasty, government of 27, 53, 56, 57, 59–61, 63, 65–67, 69–71, 73, 79, 80, 93, 98
Qiu Jin 69–71, 98
Red Army 84, 88–90
Reforms 66, 67, 70
Republic of China 74
Revolt, revolution, revolutionary 34, 56, 59, 60, 65–67, 70, 71, 73, 75–77, 79–85, 87–89, 91, 92
Russia 66, 75, 76, 83, 85
Scholar, scholars 11, 14, 15, 17, 19, 33, 34, 39, 40, 51, 53, 57, 70
Servant, servants 10, 11, 13, 32, 38, 39, 41, 44, 45, 55, 63, 77, 82
Shaman, shamans 10
Shandong 33, 74
Shang dynasty 7–11, 13, 14, 19, 21
Shangdong province 37
Shangguan Wan'er 34
Shanghai 43, 74, 76, 77, 79–83, 85, 98

Index 101

Silk 8, 10, 14, 15, 19, 25–27, 35, 38, 39, 43–45, 47, 64
Silk Road 44, 45
Slave, slaves 9, 10, 38, 39, 66, 97
Soldier, soldiers 8, 9, 11, 34, 40, 41, 47, 60, 61, 63–65, 67, 69, 77, 82–84, 87–90
Song dynasty 27, 37–41, 50
Songjiang 43, 45, 46
Soong Ailing 80, 81
Soong, Charlie 79–80
Soong Meiling 80, 83
Soong Qingling 79–85, 90, 98
Spring and Autumn Period 11
Students 15, 19, 22, 70, 71, 73–75, 77, 80, 81, 91, 93
Sun Yatsen 70, 71, 73–75, 79–85
Suzhou 55
Taiping, Taiping Rebellion 59–61, 64, 69, 71
Taiwan 52, 69, 85
Taizong 25, 26, 31
Tang, Tang dynasty 23, 25, 27–29, 31, 33, 34, 37, 50, 52, 98
Three Obediences 18
Tibet 25–28
Tongzhi 65–66
Tribute 26, 37
Turks 26
Upper class 27, 31, 37–40, 49, 50, 70, 82
War 9–11, 13, 26, 27, 37, 46, 56, 59–61, 65, 66, 69, 74, 80, 84
Warlord 74–76, 80–82
Warring States Period 11–13
Weave, weaving 14, 15, 17, 18, 21, 28, 38, 39, 43–47, 49
Widow, widows 13–15, 51, 52, 64, 82–84
Wife, wives 9, 11, 13, 17, 18, 26, 32, 37–39, 40, 43, 45, 47, 56, 64, 65, 69, 81, 89, 93
Woman Liu 49–53
Women's quarters 37, 38, 40, 64
Women's writing (Nushu) 53
Wu Ding 9, 10
Wu Sangui 55–57
Wu Zetian 31–35, 98
Xi An 65
Xianfeng 65
Xiang Jingyu 73–77, 93, 98
Xupu 73
Yan'an 89–90
Yangzi River 59, 82
Yellow Emperor's Canon of Internal Medicine 22
Yin and yang 22
Yin Ruins 7, 8
Yongle (emperor) 56
Yuan dynasty 43–45, 50
Yuan Shikai 80, 81
Yunnan 57
Zhejiang 69, 70
Zhen Yuanyuan 55–57
Zheng Zhenxiang 7, 8, 98
Zhou dynasty 11, 13, 98
Zhou Enlai 85, 93, 98
Zhu De 85, 88, 89, 91–93